TWENTY-FIVE ARTISTS

TWENTY-FIVE ARTISTS

Foreword
THOMAS M. MESSER

Editor
ARLENE BUJESE

UNIVERSITY PUBLICATIONS OF AMERICA, INC.

© 1982 by University Publications of America, Inc.

Frederick, Maryland

ISBN: 0-89093-522-X.

All Photographs Copyright © by Hans Namuth

Printed in the United States of America

Table of Contents

Acknowledgements

Calvin Albert: Originally appeared in the catalogue to an exhibition of Mr. Albert's work at the Guild Hall Museum, East Hampton, New York, 1979. Copyright 1979, Guild Hall Museum.

Alice Baber: Originally appeared as "Alice Baber and the Tragedy of Light." Used with the kind permission of Mrs. James Jones.

Warren Brandt: Originally appeared as "Brandt: The Mystery of the Commonplace," *ARTnews,* March 1968, pages 38, 39, and 73. Copyright 1968, *ARTnews.*

James Brooks: Originally appeared in the catalogue to an exhibition of Mr. Brook's work at the Gruenebaum Gallery, New York, 1979. Used with the kind permission of Carter Ratcliff.

Chuck Close: Originally appeared as "Chuck Close: Decoding the Image," *Arts Magazine,* June 1968, pages 146 through 149. Copyright 1978, *Arts Magazine.*

Elaine de Kooning: Originally appeared in the announcement of an exhibition of Mrs. de Kooning's work at the Ellison Gallery, Fort Worth, Texas, 1960.

Willem de Kooning: Originally appeared as "To and About Willem de Kooning," in *Willem de Kooning Drawings* by Thomas Hess, New York Graphic Society, Greenwich, Connecticut, 1972. Used with the kind permission of Kenneth Koch, copyright 1972.

Jimmy Ernst: Originally appeared in the catalogue to an exhibition of Mr. Ernst's work at the Cologne Art Institute, Cologne, West Germany, 1963. Used with the kind permission of James Johnson Sweeney.

Audrey Flack: Originally appeared in the catalogue to an exhibition of Ms. Flack's work at the University of Southern·Florida, Tampa, 1982. Used with the kind permission of Dr. Linnea Dietrich.

Balcomb Greene: Originally appeared as "Literary Balcomb Greene," *Review of Contemporary Fiction,* October 1982, pages 99 through 101. Used with the kind permission of Coleman Dowell, author of *White on Black on White,* to be published this spring.

Howard Kanovitz: Originally appeared as part of "Howard Kanovitz: Painter of Contradiction," in the catalogue to an exhibition of Mr. Kanovitz's work at the Academie der Kunste, West Berlin, 1979. Used with the kind permission of Jorn Merkert. Translated by David Rattray.

William King: Originally appeared in the catalogue to an exhibition of Mr. King's work at the Terry Dintenfass Gallery, New York, 1970. Copyright 1970, Terry Dintenfass, Inc.

Lee Krasner: Originally appeared as "An American Great: Lee Krasner," *Vogue,* June 1972, pages 118 through 120. Copyright 1972. Courtesy *Vogue* by The Conde Nast Publications Inc. Used with the kind permission of Barbara Rose.

Ibram Lassaw: Originally appeared as "The Sculpture of Ibram Lassaw," in the catalogue to an exhibition of Mr. Lassaw's work at the Gertrude Kalle Gallery, Detroit, Michigan, 1968. Used with the kind permission of Sam Hunter, author of the forthcoming book, *Arnoldo Pomodoro,* by Abbeville Press.

John Little: Originally appeared as part of "John Little: A Retrospective Exhibit of Works from 1934–1982," the catalogue to an exhibition of Mr. Little's work at the Guild Hall Museum, East Hampton, New York, 1982. Copyright 1982, Guild Hall Museum.

Conrad Marca-Relli: Originally appeared in the preface for *Marca-Relli* by Harold Rosenberg, Ediciones Polygrafa/SA, Barcelona, Spain, 1976. Co-edition, Rizzoli International, New York, 1976. Copyright 1976, Ediciones Polygrafa/SA.

Robert Motherwell: Used with the kind permission of Mr. Motherwell. Translated by Jack Fram.

Alfonso Ossorio: Originally appeared in *Contem-*

porary Artists, edited by Colin Naylor and Genesis P-Orridge, St. Martin's Press, New York, 1977. Copyright 1977, St. Martin's Press.

Larry Rivers: Originally appeared as "A Memoir by Frank O'Hara" in the catalogue to an exhibition of Mr. Rivers's work in which the text was by the artist and the introduction by Sam Hunter. The exhibition was at the Rose Art Museum, Brandeis University, Waltham, Masachusetts, which kindly extended the use of this material.

Alexander Russo: Used with the kind permission of Sheldon Harnick.

George Segal: Originally appeared in the catalogue to an exhibition of Mr. Segal's work at the Sidney Janus Gallery, New York, 1965. Used with the kind permission of Mr. Sidney Janis.

Syd Solomon: Originally appeared as "Syd Solomon in 1978" in the catalogue to an exhibition of Mr. Solomon's work at the Art and Culture Center, Hollywood, Florida, 1978. Used with the kind permission of John MacDonald.

Esteban Vicente: Originally appeared as "Vicente Paints a Collage," *ARTnews,* September 1953, pages 38 through 40, and 51. Copyright 1953, *ARTnews.*

Jack Youngerman: Originally appeared as "An Interview with Jack Youngerman: The New Sculpture," *Arts Magazine,* December 1975, pages 90 and 91. Copyright 1975, *Arts Magazine.*

The cooperation and generosity of a number of galleries, publications, and individuals have been instrumental in the successful compilation of this publication and the exhibition planned for December of 1982. Each of the works of art had to be reserved well in advance so that the exhibition would parallel the pictorial aspects of the publication.

The loan of works and photographs from the following galleries is greatly appreciated: Leo Castelli Gallery, Terry Dintenfass, Inc., Fischbach Gallery, Xavier Fourcade, Inc., Gruenebaum Gallery, Sidney Janis Gallery, M. Knoedler & Co., Inc., Marlborough Gallery, Louis K. Meisel Gallery, and Pace Editions, Inc.

In addition to providing the photographs which in effect were the inspiration for this project, Hans Namuth has been most generous in terms of time, advice, and patience. Without his cooperation, the idea could not have come to fruition. Many thanks to the artists, who responded with enthusiasm, encouragement, and—most of all—generosity. Thanks also to the artists' assistants and gallery assistants who helped coordinate written materials and works of art; and, finally, UPA editor Leslie Le Blanc for her tireless efforts in tracking down all the loose ends and tying them together.

Foreword

TWENTY-FIVE ARTISTS—photographer Hans Namuth and twenty-four artists—is an anniversary exhibition for Phoenix II in Washington, D.C. Quite appropriately, the occasion honors the gallery through artists without whom the place would have no raison d'être. We may begin, therefore, with the three columns of eight painters and sculptors referred to in the title, but discard as quickly as possible the arbitrary alphabetical sequence in favor of one that would provide a clue for a conceptual justification. As we attempt this, and as our name-bound minds jump from Abstract Expressionism to Photo-Realism, associations with The Springs and other places in the Hamptons begin to mingle with Provincetown, Lower Manhattan and Peggy Guggenheim, to empty eventually into a sea of ideas, images, and forms that are without attachment to externals and without need to be identified, the reassuring categories, with their comfortable sense of orderliness that are normally at our disposal, are of little use here, whether by grouping generations, isms, or geography. Yet in those cross-currents that provide nothing graspable at first, there is a unifying view just the same—one that may be gleaned through the photographer's lens.

And a keen lens it is, as is the eye behind it. Through it we see Balcomb Greene like a King Canute, immovably entrenched within his thought that reduces the sea behind him to a mere metaphor. Lee Krasner, very tall, arises dominantly above her brushes. Larry Rivers in a moment of crucial decision, his keen kinetic intelligence isolated within the immobility of the studio. A youthful Jack Youngerman, sharp and lean against the hard edges of a painting. George Segal viewing a naked body with a sexless detachment of a professional form maker. Howard Kanovitz expressionless in contrast with a painted woman's face where everything is brought to the surface. Yes, and Alice Baber, as most of us have never seen her and none of us ever will again, her lovely features attenuated but still intact, her head held and contained within a metal halo vest, as she deploys her pure and exquisite artistry against the cancer in a last, gallant rear-guard action since overpowered. These and many others are the photographic interpretations that Hans Namuth has created for us on this occasion, thereby providing the exhibition and the book that accompanies it with an armature that otherwise would be lacking.

But the twenty-four painters and sculptors whose likenesses have become the medium in the sight of an exceptionally gifted photographer/artist can hardly be asked to forego their own choice on this occasion. They exercise this choice through the selection of a favorite work and that of a favorite published comment about themselves. Each of the twenty-four artists is thus presented three-fold. Through the work of his or her choice, through an insight given literary form, and through photographic interpretation, the artist's persona is reflected in a selected work (and its reproduction on the printed page), and is reinforced by mirror images conveyed through Hans Namuth's perception, as well as through printed commentaries that conjure up literary analogies to visual experience.

Let us read some of them as we extract some highlights from the full versions quoted in the pages of this book:

No better way to begin than with perhaps the most loyal publicist of *The New American Painting,* Tom Hess, who summed up Elaine de Kooning's contribution as follows: "Certain artists, as a premise, censor chaos and establish clarity from the word 'go.' Elaine de Kooning is foolhardy enough to invite chaos in and to fight it every inch of the way to a gasp of truth. The paintings are marked by the struggle and its risks. But because they have been opened to risk and chaos, they are literate, able to speak, to doubt, question, attack, despair, affirm. ..."

Praise by a fellow artist tends to be the hardest to come by and therefore the most precious, as Calvin Albert indicates by choosing as his favorite lines those by Balcomb Greene: "He moves with apparent ease between abstraction and representation—a figure leaning in the wind, a figure reclining, each more alive than the other, each more real."

Alfonso Ossorio, himself much praised by artists, chooses to air key aspects of critical evaluation of his work when he refers to Jane Bell's article from which he quotes the first paragraph: "During a career that has spanned three decades, Ossorio's work has been approached critically from two viewpoints, neither of which is incorrect but rather overlapping. First, he has been historically placed among the first generation of Abstract Expressionists, supported by Ossorio's close enduring friendship with Jackson Pollock, whose influence can indeed be seen in the surrealist ink drawings Ossorio produced during the 1940s. Second, much has been rightly made of the artist's relationship with French artist Jean Dubuffet, whose abiding fascination with *Art Brut* ("raw art") closely paralleled Ossorio's, if it did not precisely influence it. Ossorio's development has incorporated these elements into his work—but it is not, as has been suggested, derivative of it."

"John Little's art is incisive," writes Judith Wolfe, and she continues to characterize it: "It crackles with intelligence and bold variety. It also plays a role in one of the most fascinating periods of American art, in which a generation came into contact with the European avant-garde artistic movements of the first third of the century and wrested from this experience a body of distinctive, large-scale abstract works of highly individual styles."

And John D. MacDonald, rephrasing and simplifying an overcomplex, earlier homage, (in 1978) would speak of Syd Solomon by stating straightforwardly that: "These paintings have a surface accessibility. They have a handsome look. They glow. They decorate. But they are talking another language at the same time, far less accessible, almost inaudible. It is a gut language of ancient visceral symbols. When both these idioms are accessible to the viewer, they pull and push against each other, reacting in such a way that great tension is produced, and there is a simultaneous intellectual-emotional reaction."

Let the poets have the last word as they versify about their admired counterparts Robert Motherwell and Willem de Kooning.

El negro motherwell,
Motherwell's black, his Spanish Elegies, are Rafael Alberti's theme which he carries through stanzas clearly meant to be read aloud in Spanish, to its patriotically grandiloquent conclusion:

Por el motherwell negro España libre negro
Pobre España.

Finally, Kenneth Koch provides the verses "To and About Willem de Kooning," praising him as "One of the greatest painters in America," attributing to him, still in verse-prose

"... independence
Of every stroke and shred of color, while
The whole thing held together with such style..."

and ending in a manner distinctly applicable to those rash enough to embark upon introductory embellishments:

"Can one even
Write prefaces for such?"
he asks.
"It's too demanding.
I cannot do Bill justice—too much lateness
On my part, and on his too much sheer greatness."

Artists are mirrored in their likenesses and bespoken by those who seek to pay them homage, but ultimately it is the painting or the sculpture itself that must speak and each does so partly in its own behalf, partly as an example selected by the artist to evoke many of the works buried in our more or less acute memories. Esteban Vicente's *Blue Band* thus recalls many of the paintings informed by the same coloristic mastery and sureness of hand. Ibram Lassaw's gilded *Metagalaxy* tells us something about the integration of structure and ritual; while Jimmy Ernst, ever an image-seeker, attains delicate balances between explicit and subsumed content in *Illumination for an Absent Friend. Runge*, by James Brooks, is a powerful testimony to this painter's continued capacity to use color as a shaping form element and, beyond this, his capacity to imbue it with strong communicative content that is no less compelling for being non-verbal. Conrad Marca-Relli's untitled collage, and other such works, creates forceful superimpositions revealing productive tensions between spontaneity and control, while reminding us how coloristic reductivity can paradoxically lead to an enhanced sense of richness. *Age of Ontological Crisis*, by Alexander Russo, places his masses of humanity within a cosmic context, while Warren Brandt's ostensibly primitive *Resting Model* or William King's whimsically humorous *Wallflower* strike opposite cords. Finally, both Audrey Flack and Chuck Close express themselves through an updated idiom—one in *What She Is*, through the interpretation of high kitsch, the other by submitting the language of forms to detailed and undisguised analysis in a revealing *Self-Portrait.*

Phoenix II may therefore congratulate itself for having attracted such manifold talent and for having recruited Hans Namuth to impose his own sensibility upon the gathering. Many happy returns!

Thomas M. Messer, Director
The Solomon R. Guggenheim Foundation

Hans Namuth

Interview

Q: What was it that motivated you, what inspired you, to photograph *artists* thirty or more years ago?

A. Inspiration had little to do with it; the hazards of my profession did.

Q: Does the artist differ as a subject from other people?

A. Yes, he is different. He wears his inner thoughts and vibrations on his face (as does the poet); he doesn't conceal them. He is mostly free in front of the camera and, in a sense, uninhibited. A true artist will always make a good picture—if he lets you.

Q: What prompts you to initiate a photographic session with certain artists? Is it the person? The work? And what if you don't like either?

A. To answer your first question, it is usually an assignment that takes me to an artist. And if I don't like either artist or work, or if there is no *atom crochu* as the French call it, no rapport of any sort, it may well happen that I fold my camera and leave.

Q: Do you discourage "posing"? What do you do if the artist is at work?

A. Oh, I don't discourage anything. I often let the artist take over and let *him* take the picture, so to speak. Thus, a "posed" picture can turn out to be very good. Furthermore, I don't disturb an artist at work. I welcome it when this happens, and often take photographs during a work session. This means, of course, that you established a very special relation-ship with that artist. Mark Rothko never let me be present when he was working, for good reasons. But others did; some seemed to welcome me or pretend not to see me. I immediately feel at home upon entering an artist's place. Sooner or later something develops. And the best direction is an absence of direction, a certain aloofness which is in reality charged with energy.

Q: Do your own feelings of the moment affect your work?

A. Unfortunately, yes. I remember my visit to Joan Miro in Mallorca some years ago. As he greeted me at the door he informed me that the friend who had brought us together had just died. I was so shaken that the pictures I took that day turned out not to be among my best, although Miro was most gracious and gave me all the time in the world.

Q: What interferes most while you are working?

A. Intruders.

Q: What has been the most challenging situation for you as a photographer?

A. There were several. The one that comes to mind most vividly was meeting James Thurber in Connecticut. A magazine editor and I rang the bell to his house at the appointed hour, and we heard Thurber's slow, shuffling steps coming to the door. As he opened it (knowing who we were but not seeing us because he was nearly blind), he said: *"We have* photographers as other people have *mice!*" I had a strong urge to leave at that point, to forget about the assignment, but I stayed on. After an hour or so of talk, he had mellowed considerably. He said to me, "I would like you to have my latest book." I was stunned—the author of *The Male Animal* greatly admired by me, offering this noble gesture of friendship! He reached for the book (which turned out to be *My Years with Ross,* just about to be published) and started inscribing it to me very carefully, asking the correct spelling of my name, etc. He then proceeded making a drawing of a dog's face, holding the book close to his eyes, and he then handed it to his wife who, very matter-of-factly—as if she had done this every day (and probably had)—added the dog's face and mouth. I cherish it.

Q: Have you ever had a session after which you felt the results were not worth keeping?

A. Yes.

Q: What if the artist does not like the pictures? Will you exhibit them?

A. As far as I can remember, it has never happened. When I like what I did the artist usually does, too. A story comes to mind, though. In 1979 I showed 63 large Jackson Pollock prints in Paris, at the Musée d'Art Moderne de la Ville de Paris. Pollock's widow, the artist Lee Krasner, was interviewed at that time by the Paris correspondent of the *New York Times.*

She mentioned that my photographs of Pollock made him look *grim.* She said, as I recall it, that Pollock's stern look was only a small part of him—and not the whole man—that he had a wide smile. She also quoted Susan Sontag's thought that photographers project their own image when they're supposed to be showing reality.

This raised a number of thoughts and questions in my mind. Does an artist ever not look "grim"—intense would be a better word—when he is working? Would he smile during the "creative process"? And am I really projecting myself when I photograph others? To the contrary, I feel that I am rather self-effacing during a photographic session. I become an echo. It is true, of course, that the camera, lights, et cetera, get in the way, and I sometimes wish that all the paraphernalia would disappear. There is a fairy tale about a cap that makes a person who wears it invisible—a photographer's dream!

Q: Speaking of Susan Sontag, have you read her book *On Photography*?

A. Yes, I think her book *On Photography* is stimulating and infuriating. But it is full of great quotes. I found a statement by Richard Avedon which applies to our discussion: "The pictures have a reality for me that the people don't. It is through the photographs that I know them," and Sontag herself writes this: "The whole point of photographing people is that you are not intervening in their lives, only visiting them. The photographer . . . is an extension of the anthropologist, visiting natives and bringing back news of their exotic doings and strange gear."

Q: When were the portraits in this present collection made, and how did you make your selections?

A. Between 1953 and 1982. Among the six I added this year alone was brave and beautiful Alice Baber, who just died. And when I searched my files for Jack Youngerman (I photographed him several times) I miraculously found a take I had never printed before. Most of the other portraits have not seen the light of day until now. All my choices almost imposed themselves. And to your qustion, why this particular one and not another? Why a de Kooning of almost 30 years ago and not one done now? And the Segal of 1980 and not the one taken in 1965? Do the years not count? Are these the same people? My answer is: they are—and yet, they are not. A face changes, a person changes, as does the work. It is my belief that there is a permanent face everyone has in his or her life, to be retained in image and memory. Once this image has been extracted I don't need to go back. It took years before I came to realize this.

When I look at the 24 artists it strikes me again how serious and solemn most of them look. But art is a serious business; there is nothing lighthearted about it. People working at art all their lives have scars, you may not see them, but they do. Think of Gorky, Pollock, David Smith, Mark Rothko.

I am reminded of something Goethe said: "So bist du nun—dir kannst du nicht entrinnen." "Thus you are—you cannot escape yourself!"

October 1982

JACK YOUNGERMAN 1959

JIMMY ERNST 1958

ALICE BABER 1982

WILLEM de KOONING 1953

ELAINE de KOONING 1953

BALCOMB GREENE 1975

WILLIAM KING 1980

CONRAD MARCA-RELLI 1982

ALEXANDER RUSSO 1982

WARREN BRANDT 1982

JOHN LITTLE 1952

LEE KRASNER 1962

JAMES BROOKS 1975

CHUCK CLOSE 1981

AUDREY FLACK 1982

LARRY RIVERS 1970

ROBERT MOTHERWELL 1953

22

ALFONSO OSSORIO 1962

HOWARD KANOVITZ 1980

GEORGE SEGAL 1980

IBRAM LASSAW 1966

SYD SOLOMON 1981

ESTEBAN VICENTE 1981

CALVIN ALBERT 1982

Calvin Albert

Powerful—majestic—mysterious. To describe the work of Calvin Albert and record its effect, does not add to it. To trade in comparisons and place him at the very top of his contemporaries (though pleasant to do) reduces art to competition, to a game. It is significant that he has found the most difficult, and yet the most meaningful, course possible for an artist today.

He moves with apparent ease between abstraction and representation—a figure leaning in the wind, a figure reclining, each more alive than the other, each more real. In times of great uncertainty in art (as outside it) the safe and profitable stance is a fixed position, anchorage upon a presumed opposite. Abstraction *or* realism. Good against evil. Them versus us. But has one actually made a choice?

The young artist, rejecting the extremes and their simplification, may *decide* that the good thing, the future and success is a return to the great men of our early century: Matisse, Picasso, Braque, Giacometti, to walk with nimble mind and feet this dangerous abstraction—realism road.

But in art one cannot calculate.

You have or you don't have the vision and the necessity, like Calvin Albert, to face the complexities, the dangers and the never satisfying rewards of life against death.

Balcomb Greene
1979

Alice Baber

I have watched the development of this remarkable painter with a close eye and closer intellectual interest over a period of about eight years. It is the first time (and so far, the only time) I have had the opportunity to study the interior development of a serious, good painter from almost the moment of new inception. I consider myself lucky to have had such an opportunity.

Alice Baber says of the beginnings of the development in her painting which has led to her present work, that she wanted to dominate still-lifes because they would not accept gratuitous light. The particular painting was one she called *Battle of the Oranges,* and she was trying to find "a way to get the light moving across the whole thing"—without having to rely on the conventional view, the traditional values of negative space and positive space. She was working in cadmium red, cadmium orange, cadmium yellow, light and medium (all, one notes, sun colors), and the space between the oranges suddenly came alive. And as it did, the spatial relationships between the oranges became agitated, somehow no longer fixed, hence the title. It was for her the painting in which she departed from subject matter and moved toward a more personal image, personal metaphor.

From these first, very precious and different oranges, she moved along to working in two-dimensional circles of light, an attempt to give transparency so as to see more than one thing at one time. It was still the light she was after, from behind, from before, from within, simultaneous total luminosity. Again she changed, to avoid the geometric trap of overlapping circles. Her shapes became less and less unrecognisable as "shapes." At this time dark colors began to appear with more and more frequency. Her balls and discs of pure color were still there from time to time, now often all floating in space of total black, or totally unrelated to each other in the midst of swirling darks. Some of the increasingly abstract canvases of this period are so deeply sad and full of total gloom of darks as to be almost unbearable to view.

It is hard to believe all this, looking at the new work. It is as though Alice Baber deliberately and consciously sank herself into all these blacks and deep deep darks in order to learn and come back with what she needed in her continued pursuit of and study of light. She is, really is, after all, a color painter. And she has now found a way to make her darks peculiarly *color: color* in themselves rather than *values* in a chiaroscuro scale. And of all her lights, her airy jewel-like colors have acquired new, strangely 'darker' values within themselves as well.

First off, for myself, I must say that I think Alice Baber is a painter with a very strong, very basic tragic sense. I myself think she could not tolerate the triteness of painting sorrow in the conventional way; that she wanted more than that; that she wanted to paint sorrow in light gay colors, as nature does. This may sound strange, looking at all these lovely, laughing, brilliant colors she uses. But in looking closer one can see and feel an almost terrifying poignancy, a near weeping sadness and sorrow in these delicately gay and summer-bright colors. It is as if she is trying to tell us about her native Illinois, with its brilliant blinding sun, its dust, its summer-deep greens, that Summer itself will not stay. School *must* begin again. Grandmothers and oldsters will not last the Winter. One feels a strange choking sorrow over the gay beauty she shows us, one does not feel gay or abandoned.

All of this did not come about by accident, as I have pointed out, and in her continued study of light and the tragedy of light, Alice Baber has brought to us now a kind of 'celestial painting.'

It is as if she wanted to get away from the Earth (and from her Spirit) to another Reality. Perhaps a better one. Or perhaps a personal *rearrangement* of Reality. This is Tragic, because it is impossible. But what she gives us is a hint, a vague image of what light might be, on some other universe. The 'Tragedy' is, of course, that light out in spaces does not exist, of and by itself. Light to be seen at all must strike, be reflected from an object. An object implies a third party: light, the viewer—and a reflecting element. In our lives, then, light can't even be seen alone. This is the tragedy of light, and Alice Baber understands it.

James Jones
1963

Warren Brandt

One can say this—Warren Brandt borders on dangerous ground: illustration and the intimate scene. The former is the art of the story-teller; the latter, a sentimentality out of familiar and beloved environment. What saves him from a possible depressing banality is a detached and cool perspective which relates to art. His love of painting, his solid background in all its phases, his exploration of forms that he is temperamentally allied to—all these tend to give substance to his recent painting. There are two possibilities in art; one is to react against the past, the other to continue traditional concepts; to carry a thread of the past, however wavering (there is no single tradition in Western art as there was in China), into one's work, whether by subject or form.

As I have suggested, Warren Brandt's painting starts with a realism dangerously close to illustration. It is his way. Once the step has been taken—he has a sure eye for his failings—he proceeds methodically to destroy it, to make it over. A romantic conception? Perhaps. But it takes nerve to destroy what comes easy. Facility can be used, but it can use one too. Whatever is left of the first tracings is blurred or obliterated or incorporated as a substructure, unintelligible as markings found on city streets. Brandt does not talk about "being original," a twentieth-century malaise that does more harm than good. Whether he intends it or not, a certain anonymity exists. His reverence for the past, which does not deny the contributions of the twentieth century, as I will suggest later, and his preference for one artist over another, have contributed to his maturity. Certain painters send him reeling; Matisse, for instance. No need to cover that up; it is self-evident. Why Matisse? Well, perhaps his years in Paris. Certainly his love of color. The use of the intimate theme—the nude, a book, a table, a chair that swings out of the corner of the picture, a couch, an open door. Brandt loves everything lived in, touched, used, sat on, leaned on; in other words, the commonplace.

Colette, in *Break of Day*, speaks of love and maternal instinct as the two great commonplaces. But what commonplaces! With Brandt, no object is assigned an inferior place. Each has its fixed position, its purpose, its meaning in the ensemble. Proustian, in that they recall something remembered. This does not mean that it is literature any more than Jackson Pollock's great painting, *Scent,* has a smell. An object may be a swatch of color, a quick stroke of the brush signifying an object, a form cut out of scraped underpainting. It is a putting on, a taking off, an openmindedness for the infinite possibility. This approach to painting could very well have come out of his involvement with the Abstract-Expressionists in the '50s and early '60s. He was a frequent visitor to the "Club" where most of the major painters of that movement met. For a while he was seriously concerned with their ideas, but eventually he found that they did not suit him temperamentally. However, they did release him from fixed concepts and opened new ways of approach that became clearer to him. In his latest work some of the freedom, the chanciness of choice, has been more evident, particularly in his smaller paintings. Color in his new paintings has gained over drawing, his first love. In earlier work he was able to pull out of a difficult situation by depending on his abilities as a draftsman. His new work is constructed by color. He cuts through objects and space, letting them become one. He destroys the literal plane and forces the color to assume both space and object. More and more his work tends towards the abstraction that is so absorbing in a Matisse. It is a real abstraction because it comes out of things and is an invention. It does not exist except in the mind. It has no use except pleasure. Perhaps like love, and other inventions, it has become old-fashioned, but it has its place along with other and more recent manifestations.

Two teachers influenced his formative years, Philip Guston and Max Beckmann. It was Max Beckmann, with his illustrative abilities, his profound consciousness of traditional forces, his European sophistication, who influenced him most. Certain facilities that could possibly harm him as an artist might, he could now see, be put to purposeful use. In Paris, where he lived for a while, his work took on a strong Beckmannesque quality, which he worked at until it had run its course, like a fever. French art intrigued him. Its formal arrangements, its abstractness, its inventiveness—in other words, the art of it.

It was during that period that his work began to change. The earlier influences began to fade away and something unsuspected—color—began to play its important role in his painting.

Herman Cherry
1968

James Brooks

James Brooks is known as a pioneer of the New York School, a first-generation innovator. These labels grant him his historical significance, yet they can be misleading. At the very least, they can distract us from the fundamental value of his art. No serious painter paints in order to become part of history. He paints in order to convey meanings he considers important. Nonetheless, we can follow art history's leads to vantage points where some of those meanings come into view.

Take the matter of Jackson Pollock's automatism—his drip painting. The technique appeared in 1947. By the following season it had energized Brooks's own work, giving him a way to break free from constricted (that is, Cubist) styles of drawing, of imagining form in pictorial space. Brooks's supercharged expressiveness still flows from the freedoms gained in the last few years of the 1940s. To make sense of what he has done later, some distinctions have to be made.

Jackson Pollock's dripped line is demonic, always rushing beyond itself, as if to outstrip some propelling obsession. Brooks's early dripped, poured and scraped images have a fast-moving dignity that foreshadows the elegance and energy shown by his paintings of subsequent decades. In other words, he remade Pollock's drip painting, and in the process he ran across another technique, as Hans Hofmann had done a few years before: stain painting.

Now, it has been claimed that stain painting, a natural and obvious outcome of New York School automatism, was invented in the early 1950s by Helen Frankenthaler—as if painters paint in order to be credited with the invention of techniques. Perhaps some of the color-field painters who took off from Frankenthaler's rather late staining do indeed paint for such reasons (for the sake of entering an art history reduced to a series of technical innovations), but Brooks, Hofmann, Pollock? No. Once again, the purpose of their painting is to convey important meanings.

It helps to go back to the early years of the New York School—to that welter of new ideas and methods—to get a sense of the way the search for meaning was carried on. It helps because Brooks has maintained the spirit of that search right up to the present moment. He plunged into an eruption of possibilities, drawing from it something very much like serenity. His splashed, poured, dripped line is not demonic so much as a confident groping into the very nature of paint on canvas—which is, of course, the unknown. The surprise, the shock, of these beginnings came as sheer matter generated a power beyond itself, as energized paint evoked sudden crises of feeling and insight.

Where Pollock would keep pouring, gesturing, until the image was built up to a tangled density, Brooks was—and is—more judicious. He lets the initial gesture (and the crisis it evokes) remain in view until it reveals some particular character. Then he responds with further gestures. The method is just as spontaneous as that of any other New York action painter, Pollock included, and yet it elevates spontaneity to a realm where time, the rhythm of expressive give and take across the surface of the canvas, flows more at the pace of deep evolution than of quickly changing mood. Thus the sudden skittering flourishes of line and texture that characterize Brooks's images make them reflections of his own, distinctively refined personality. At the same time, the overall impact of his paintings occurs at the scale of decades, of eras. He is a painter of our times, post-war America, not a painter of fleeting moments.

Each image begins in a flash of jagged chaos, and that event is never suppressed. Nor is the ground where the event occurs. Brooks primes his canvases in black, and the colors generated out of that non-color are often cold and harsh. Warmth is felt in painterly gesture, which reads first as a sign of sheer energy: paint reaches and spreads as if it were capable of gesture itself. Reaching, it forms boundaries—between a stark white floating presence, for example, and the depths of a bluish off-white. Or deep blues move across the original void, the black prime coat, covering most of it, leaving scraps to drift beneath an overlay of white and vermillion.

As form curves, leaps, balloons, tenses to leap again, it pushes scale up while inviting the opposite of painterly form: geometry. Brooks's "organisms" often inspire lines, rectangles, triangles. And his forms always develop intense relationships with that inevitable geometry, the edge of the canvas. As a result, energy learns stability. Explosiveness is transformed into calm, though never absorbed by it. Both qualities remain. An abiding purpose of abstraction is to permit just such complexity, and to encourage wide-ranging responses.

There is, for example, great pleasure to be taken in the sheer lushness of Brooks's paint surfaces and in the intricacies of his forms. His art can also be seen as a struggle between those torrential, primordial powers loosed by his first gesture and the elegance, the refined self-awareness, that appears subsequently in nuances of adjustment and balance. The way explosiveness and calm coexist in Brooks's paintings gives them a further meaning, for each is a fully intended instance of complexity in the face of ordinary life's power to suppress the complex, to enforce imagistic simplicities. Brooks's art can be seen as a critique of our period's bland, mechanistic approaches to difficulties in art and elsewhere.

This critique is of the most generous kind, for it takes the form of counter-examples. Brooks offers a dazzling exuberance as an alternative to stiltedness. Inspiration is put in the place of caution. It ought to be pointed out that he makes no such claim for his art. His stated purpose is to paint as well as he can. If the results seem to point beyond themselves, to offer a commentary on the larger world, it is the viewer's responsibility to notice. The sheer richness of Brooks's painting makes it a responsibility difficult to pass up.

Carter Ratcliff
1979

Chuck Close

"One of the things that put me off about even the word realism was that I didn't have any idea what the hell it meant. I know in literature what it means as opposed to romanticism or whatever, but how can you spend a year making something and know whether it has anything to do with reality? I mean I'm so involved constantly with the artificiality of what I'm doing," Chuck Close commented recently.[1]

When those gigantic heads of his first appeared a decade ago—like Athena out of the brow of Zeus—it was their realism that stunned us. Photographic verity, deadpan reproduction, imitation of nature (by way of the illusionistic surface of a black and white snapshot) were startlingly new, and everyone assumed their derivation from Pop Art.[2]

Now that we are used to photographic realism and art has gone on to other fictions,[3] it is the artificialities of Close's work that speak to us. It is the extreme scale and the underlying concern with identity that keep his work current, and the ambivalent involvement with Minimalist principles that informs us about our own recent past. For now, ten years later, the minimal aspects of his artificial realism have become increasingly apparent: his work is grounded in a reductive, formal, abstract orientation. The mammoth frontal heads against neutral grounds are images as static and iconic, as isolated and literal, as any Minimalist cube.

To begin with, his attitude toward materials is literal and reductive. The black and white heads that he started painting in 1967 were the result of "a long process of increasing the self-imposed limitations in my work," he wrote in a statement a few years ago. "I had arrived at a process that allowed me to minimize the amount of paint employed to make an image in the full gray scale of the photograph. I had reduced the evidence of my hand to a minimum . . . I limited my color to black." A tablespoon of paint was enough for a nine-by-seven-foot canvas.

When his work suddenly burst into living color in 1971, the increase in reality was disappointing—the photographic artificiality seemed lost, the duplicity of the image diminished. But it was through an equally minimal and even more artificial process: he was using only the three basic colors of the printing process ("they're not three colors you can care a lot about"), one at a time. "I found that when I was just using black it all happened on the canvas, there was no palette. So when I started making color paintings I wanted that same sort of thing to happen with the colors specifically mixed in context on the canvas. So that's why I went to the bizarre lengths of getting color separations and making three one-color paintings on top of each other, and the color was built *in situ* where I could see what I was doing."

Meanwhile, the gridded drawings and prints that he began making a few months later, in 1972, were not only explaining the process by which the paintings were built up—block by block like a brick wall, as he says, and layer by layer like a color print—but also clarifying an attitude: seriality, modularity, and grid structure derive from Minimalism. The paintings (which he refers to as "continuous tone paintings" because they were made from dye-transfer prints—continuous tone separations, with no halftone dots) retain no evidence of a grid. In the drawings, prints, watercolors, and most recently pastels, Close lets his process show, and shows up realism as an artificial construction.

Faces dissolve into dots and squares; circles in a grid coalesce into heads. As if pressed behind a screen, trapped within the warp and woof of a tapestry or the tesserae of a Roman mosaic, the image is bracketed by unreality, distanced by design, flickering through the mesh of a grid. It is reduced to a pattern. The realism is a matter of a code, a system of simple marks, units repeated over and over. The surface is like a computerized screen transmitting an image; it has as much in common with the electronically screened images of television, which also present an iconic and repeatable reality, as with textile or mosaic. Close's paintings have often been described in landscape terms as terrains. His gridded drawings are more like the Viking photos of Mars—computer scans of an unfamiliar surface. Warhol, at the end of the machine age, wanted to be a machine; Close, a few years later when cybernetic technology was taking over, mimicked electronics and computerized his hand-made art. But being human, he could play with his own predetermined programs.

His work is full of decisions to minimize. But though he repeats the same images ("I like the idea of recycling images"), returns to the same photos, and, when interviewed, says he tends to slide into the same pre-recorded answers, the code is variable. A new watercolor neatly exposes the three-color separation process in horizontal bands, stressing the abstraction of making an image. At the bottom, the chin area is all reds; across the mouth area, red and blue combine into innumerable violet tints; and the top half of the image, having had yellow added, is natural color—complete. The unexpected lushness of the color in its unnatural unfinished states is, like the recent color-drenched Flavin space, a curious revelation of romanticism in the most factual of practitioners. It parallels the new wide range of pure unmixed color of Close's new pastels, in which he seemingly reverses the limitations of his color process and uses unlimited color—as a dot rather than a layer on paper tinted with watercolor.

"It's the antithesis of using only three colors," he says. "Now I have as many colors as I can possibly have, and instead of making the color that you want out of the three stupid colors, try and sort through all these boxes." The dots of the pastels are like a color adaptation of the tonal dots in his ink and graphite drawings, and indeed, one of the new pastels, a self-portrait, abstains from color. In neutral tones of gray and tan, made from a black and white photo, it is like a color reproduction of a black and white image: all that remains are warm and cool tones—the color is barely there. Close's colors have tended to be neutralized, grayed down, with "a kind of cancelled intensity." His new self-portrait etching uses a different code, one appropriate to the medium: the marks within its grid squares are diagonal lines, simple little scratches that recall the traditional diagonal hatching technique of Old Master etchings. And some of his newest drawings are made with fingerprints.

A few years ago Robert Bechtle commented that Close was more like LeWitt and the systemic artists than like other Photo Realists. Close equivocates:

"Well, the grid is an incredibly flexible device. I mean when you think of all the different people who have used grids for centuries, it's less locked into one stylistic point of view than practically any convention that I can think of. It's a way to break things down." Nevertheless, in the late '60s, the grid had become inextricably linked to Minimalism. If Chuck Close and Malcolm Morley adopted the grid for representational purposes, it was because the arbitrary process—methodical in Close's case, capricious in Morley's—equalized the surface, neutralized the subject matter, and invalidated the distinction between abstract and figurative. It was the same kind of tactic as making the photograph the real subject of the painting so that illusionistic space was available on a surface that remained literally flat. The resulting image, though apparently realistic, could be arrived at by purely literal processes, acceptable on Minimalist terms.

"Sometimes I laugh because to make a painting is such a long and involved process. I'll spend three weeks gessoing a canvas—ten coats—getting it all sanded and getting it perfect and it reminds me of those motel signs, 'if you lived here you'd be home now'—if I were Ryman I'd be done. And then I spend another two weeks getting a fine pencil grid and if I were Agnes Martin I'd be done and then I've got ten more months of work to do."

If his elaborate grid systems suggest LeWitt, with numbers and letters sometimes charting the edges of the image, graphlike, and titles that refer to the number of dots in the image, other references to earlier modernists can be found in his work. His 1972 mezzotint of *Keith*, exhibited at MOMA as a serial image in various darkening stages of completion, internalized the grid, building a head in close tones out of large, dark, blocky squares that seemed to contain memories of Ad Reinhardt's black paintings. His drawings that exist in series of four, with their explosive increases in the size of the central gridded rectangle and the concomitant shrinking of the framing edge as the size of the paper remains constant, seem to parody Albers' concerns. Close, who studied at Yale among Albers' disciples, denies being influenced by Albers, "unless it's unconscious. It was pretty hard to take that stuff seriously by the time it had been passed on," he says.

Giacometti also comes to mind. The smallest image, in those serial progressions of four, is the size of a postage stamp in the middle of a vast field of white paper; its indistinct reduction of the head to a blur of only 154 dots recalls Giacometti's tiny matchstick figures which also resulted from reductive investigations of perception. And the exploratory relationship between the central image of the head and the framing paper may have as much to do with

Giacometti's drawings of heads as with Albers' squares, but where Giacometti made visible all the uncertainties and insecurities of the experience of perceiving, Close presents his decisions prefabricated, and transfers the processes of perception to the viewer who unwittingly translates the gridded dots into a face, decoding the image. The tendency prevalent in the late '60s to expose the process by which a work was made was not just a return to an earlier involvement with process that had been rejected at the height of Minimalism. It was a new interpretation of the meaning of process. Where artists in the '50s had presented their work as the result of a process—the painting being the remains, the relic of an activity—the newer artists presented process as an ongoing element of the work, something that often, in conceptualist and earth works as well as Close's heads, continued after the work itself was finished.

The idea of building an image out of repeatable units has origins in the repetitive formal concerns of the '60s. In popular imagery it goes back further. On his wall, Close has an old photograph that is an image of an eagle. But the eagle is built out of hundreds of people (nurses as light tones, soldiers as dark) massed together, shot in inverse perspective from an oblique angle. "Where there might be ten people per square inch at the bottom of the image, it would take a hundred people per square inch at the top," Close points out. It is easy to see why he likes the picture: those tiny people, with their repeated heads, are like the repeated dots that build a head in his own work. It also raises the issue of scale.

Size began to be flexible early in the century. Measurability was a concern from Duchamp's three stoppages of Morris' rulers, hinting at immeasurability. It followed out of art's concern with locating objects in space, fixing them to a surface. Scale has been a puzzling issue ever since the unconscious became a deliberate element in art. It is a primary childhood source of confusion because a growing child's own scale is always changing; fantasy as well as Surrealism is full of tricks played with scale, from Jack and the beanstalk to ancient legends of primordial giants. Chuck Close's gigantic heads are purely factual, but their scale magnifies every pore, every imperfection. People see themselves that way in make-up mirrors, under harsh fluorescent light, but we rarely see each other so clearly. With so much detail, such acute focus, the eye and the camera lens become commingled; those big heads have a myopic clarity on the verge of dissolving, as if seen from the nearest point before becoming unfocused, like kissing with your eyes open. The gridded drawings dissemble as if dehydrated, as if space could be extracted at will, and reassemble, the component data taking on the lineaments of reality. Like other recent art that stretches beyond space into the realm of time or shrinks to invisibility, the space in Close's work is like an energy field emanating from the surface. His magnification and reduction—from heads nine feet high to those of an inch or two—go beyond understandable scale to extremes of scale—sliding and elastic. Magritte's shaving brush that filled a bedroom is newly relevant, not only in relation to Close's brobdingnagian hair follicles, but because it can show us that magnification and miniaturization are really the same thing: ways of dealing with an expanded and shifting scale. Their aims are the same—altering the size to get more into the same space, to cover more ground, to stretch the possibilities. Close's attitude is not unlike that of a miniaturist making a model that contains every detail.

The theme of identity has always been imbedded in his portrait heads. From the beginning, critics commented that they looked like passport photos. Frontal and slightly uncomfortable against a blank background, warts and all, their only purpose—like a passport photo—was to identify. Confronted by those magnified faces, you were reduced to the observation of minutiae, details—a glossy eyeball, a crooked tooth, a curving shadow. For what else can you say about an expressionless face? It has pores, hairs, wrinkles, blemishes. Instead of a skin of paint, Close reduced the painted surface to transparency and gave us the surface of a face; he gave us—literally—skin, and the imperfections of that realistic surface were more significant than any occasional accidental glint of unease. The information to be decoded had to do with focus, depth of field, lens type. The information was photographic, not psychological. As images, they were totally literal.

Identity, which in post-conceptual work often dissolves into an elaborate skein of narrative disguises and fictional appearances, remains a fragile shell in Close's portraits—nothing more than physical appearance, pure identification. Like the conceptualists, Close presents us with a neutral list of facts. For him, identity is not a question of Who, but How. How do we identify an image? How is an image built? The answer is a conceptual system. The photograph is one code, the continuous tone separation another, the dots within a screen of grid squares a further code, flexible as well as arbitrary—for a head made of 104,072 dots will obviously reveal more information than one made of a few hundred. If it is hard to stay away from the subject of technique, it is because the technique is, in a way, his content. And his form.

Now he is making drawings with fingerprints. Continuing a formalist tradition of body imprints, using his index finger as a tool and inking it on a stamp pad, he replaces the dot within the grid with a unique eccentric oval—his own fingerprint—and brings back the Abstract-Expressionist concept of the artist's hand, the signature brushstroke,[4] as an identifying mark. Another literal touch. Dark and light tones become a function of pressure, of a light or heavy touch against the paper, and what critics have often called Close's "pointillism" becomes instead a literal "tachism." The realism results from a basic act of touching, a simple pressure on the surface.

It is interesting that the two most minimal, most conceptual of the Photo Realists did not remain satisfied to keep reproducing the transparent photographic surface. Both, concerned with perception, moved toward a more tactile surface: touch took over where sight left off. While Morley buried his realism in choppy paint and increasingly eccentric private grid schemes, Close reduces his images to coded information, and personalizes the code. The fingerprint brings out the issue of identity—that of the maker as well as the image. It gives added dimension to the self-portraits in which he periodically scans the surface of his own face. Close likes the idea that they can't be forged; "they can't even be restored," he says. They make realism the by-product of a unique proof of identification. What could be more artificial?

In December 1971 Hilton Kramer wrote: "The kind of work Mr. Close produces is interesting only as evidence of the kind of rubbish that follows in the wake of every turn in the history of taste." A month later Emily Genauer wrote: "At this moment I'd say that most of the new photo-realism is terrible, citing Chuck Close, Malcolm Morley, and Richard McLean ... as particularly awful examples." At the same time Barbara Rose, also rejecting the whole Photo-Realist movement as "academic in the worst sense," called Close "the best of the worst."

There was a reason the critical establishment was so hostile: they were rejecting it on modernist grounds. Barbara Rose even mentioned Close's "equivocal relationship with modernism." But now that we are beginning to see modernist art as something fast receding into history, along with formalist criticism, that equivocal relationship looks less like a return to the academic past and more like its opposite: the beginnings of a radically new attitude that was signaling a fatal threat to modernism. For the moment, it is being called post-modernism by those who acknowledge the fundamental break, and pluralism by those who don't.

To future historians, the mark of the modernist period may well be its insistence on style. And Minimalism may be the last of the modernist styles, the end of a seventy-year process of stylization and formalization. "We're obviously all tagged on to the end of the tradition of western art," comments Close. But while his premises were literal, Close, like a number of other artists—late minimal, post-minimal, conceptual—who emerged in the late '60s out of the Minimalist climate, somehow turned the reductive approach against itself, making it a means for other ends. With the whole concept of style in doubt, they made motifs of Minimalist forms, subjected them to natural forces or materials, dug them into the landscape, dematerialized them, or used them as codes, turning the imperatives of a style into voluntary patterns. Close, using information as content, substituting technique for style, moves, as if in spite of himself, beyond modernism. Photo Realism, at least in the hands of Close and Morley, now looks like another manifestation of post-Minimalist art. Conceptual realism might have been a better name for it. Close is beginning to appear to be part of a generation that had the enviable or unenviable role of straddling an abyss.[5]

Kim Levin
1978

NOTES

[1] Quotes, unless otherwise specified, are from a conversation with the artist in April, 1978.

[2] It is easy to trace Close's scale to Rosenquist or Wesselmann, his mimicry of commercial printing processes to Lichtenstein, his portrait heads to Warhol; it is also misleading—the affinities are superficial.

[3] The photograph, subject matter of the Photo Realists, became a medium for post-Conceptualists, who also followed the implications of the informal snapshot to their logical conclusion: narrative content. Photo Realism, as well as Conceptualism, paved the way for the recent re-entry of content.

[4] In the early '50s, during the Abstract-Expressionist era, Saul Steinberg had turned single fingerprints into heads in a witty double entendre about identity, and titled them *Passport Photos*, but the intent was quite different.

[5] The comparison that has been made by critics between Close's heads and late Roman portraiture, like the colossal head of Constantine, can now be seen as more than merely stylistic. The brief period of our recent past, with all its overlapping categories and conflicting ideologies, will probably remain as complex to future art historians as that of all the competing cults at the end of the Roman Empire, just before Christianity became the official religion. And Close's heads, like those staring blank-faced Romans who have been interpreted as icons of spiritual uncertainty or determination, will sustain similar readings.

Elaine de Kooning

Certain artists, as a premise, censor chaos and establish clarity from the word "go." Elaine de Kooning is foolhardy enough to invite chaos in and to fight it every inch of the way to a gasp of truth. The paintings are marked by the struggle and its risks. But because they have been opened to risk and chaos, they are literate, able to speak: to doubt, question, attack, despair, affirm . . .

To toss away (the regal gestures of Rubens, Watteau, Lautrec), talent must have been there in the first place. One has to fight virtuosity. But talent controlled, strangled and, after the sacrifice, recovered creates its unique intensity: tension and radiance, the sun in the oceans of Rubens' nudes, the flick of a turned smile that haunted Watteau, the weight of sulphur in Lautrec's night-glance.

Talent strangled and in the sacrifice recovered is what informs Elaine de Kooning's art with elegance and profundity, with a vista raised to horizons in whose sweep there is plenty of room for visual wit, the agony of invention, bombardments of true color.

Here, in this sense of distance, is the field for the energy and strength of talent, after it has fought through virtuosity and also the appalling social milieu of U.S.A. 1960 (where talent is equated with that which can be most easily exploited or sliced up by the pound). In this breadth of her art is the source of its radiance, of what a less self-conscious time called "genius."

The pictures must be glanced at, seen, combed with the eyes, felt. There are no verbal equivalents. A foreword is always a backword. But for indications:

A macadam road turns past a hill crowned with gold trees, the wind turns through road and hill, raising the falling leaves in gold candelabra of spiral,

A bull, fixed in the ritual's blanked stare, blood-masked, learns endurance from his innate genius, which is courage and the fire that demolishes him as he tosses away his life to the Moment,

The last words of an executed man: "It's O.K., it's alright,"

The hill and the bull: space in a valley for a farm filled with spinning gold; a flake of bloody gristle spinning at death; the wheel of the matador, of the horse, turning on their fixed cycle,

The bull and the hill at the moment of change: like a leaper in basketball in the instant of recoil, stretching one Gothic inch more, his jump frozen as it becomes his fall,

The arenas are filled with interior color: a flag pegged to a mirror, crimson paper near an ice-grey photograph, a blue light-struck decanter, battleship grey, mustard,

The interiors are filled with arena color: a man sits posing for a portrait and becomes a solemn laughing procession of mosses, sand whites, flags, his clothes rumpled in a stateless armor mineralized by insight on commonplace,

The geometry of anguish,

Veronica,

Riposte umber-green-white-to-orange-blue-orange-purple,

Or phrase it: hill, meadow, saint's-veil, mustard, emeralds, snapdragons, dusk?

Colors fly like pennants in a regatta moving across an island woodland, masts and tree trunks vanish in the tight spinning of leaves and flags, frozen in the artist's quick glance, fixed in ice, color on color, over-lapping, spurting from interstices of branch and spar, elbow and horn, meteor and angel.

Elaine de Kooning's pictures mark a highpoint in modern American art that only talent can reach. Their claim is to wholeness: *they include.* They include you.

Thomas B. Hess
1960

Willem de Kooning

To and About Willem de Kooning

I first met Bill de Kooning in the summer
Of ninety fifty one or was it two?
To the East Hampton art scene a latecomer
My knowledge of it grew and as it grew
I no longer replied "De Kooning, um, er,
Who's that?" His was a work which once I knew
I never wanted to or could forget—
Castelli's summer house is where we met

And where I saw his paintings first; he had
A studio next to Leo's house, on Jericho
Lane, as I recall, and worked like mad
All day, then went out riding on his bicycle
(As Levin might have done in Leningrad),
One of the greatest painters in America
My friends and I all knew, a superhuman
Draughtsman, working that year on his "Woman."

I didn't know Bill well enough to visit
Him while he worked, nor could I find a sentence
To say about his art—he was a wizard
And I a sort of sorcerer's apprentice
In words, not paints. It hit me like a blizzard,
However, what he did then: independence
Of every stroke and shred of color, while
The whole thing held together with such style

That I had never seen—besides Bellini,
Titian, Piero, Bonnard, Botticelli,
And one or two more—any one whose geni-
Us was at the same time so strong and deli-
Cate it could make me shiver. The martini
I drank at dusk with Nina, then Castelli,
With Larry, Jane, and John, and Frank O'Hara
(It was a lovely time, if not an era)

I'd finish, then another glass I'd fill—
All this time everyone was always talking
In a most animated way of Bill,
Of art, of life, of reputations. Walking
From house to beach and back again until
We felt like falling into bed and stocking

Ourselves with strength to once more grow excited
By something that we knew (and were delighted

To know) was happening, we made of art
And poetry a constant exhibition
Of our excited feelings. Did this start
With abstract painting? poems? My position
Is just to say it *was,* and a great part
Of what we felt, as powerful as fission,
Was in de Kooning's women, as it was
In his abstractions later. Well, enough

Of that first summer, which I like to think of
As lovers like to think of their first meeting,
Or thirsty travelers what they'd like a drink of,
Both past and future setting the heart beating—
Long Island days that brought me to the brink of
An understanding which was like a greeting
From all that's best in which the spirit traffics,
Like this collection of de Kooning's graphics.

How thank an artist half enough who's given
One such sensations and such understanding
Of what was not on earth and not in heaven
Before he took his brushes to the landing
And stood and made it happen? Can one even
Write prefaces for such? It's too demanding.
I cannot do Bill justice—too much lateness
On my part, and on his too much sheer greatness.

I've gone on looking at his work for years;
For me his paintings highlight every season.
Music hath charms to soothe the savage ears,
His art has beauties to derange the reason
And bring it back again, like sun, which clears
The whole earth after blinding us, releasing
New energies, grass, flowers, and trees—I mean
His work illuminates, as will be seen

By opening this book a little further
To where the work of Bill de Kooning starts.
Self-Portrait with Imaginary Brother
And then his Study for the Queen of Hearts,
An early "Woman," seated, and another,
One chiefly whole, another one in parts,

Rome, Blue and White, and Woman in a Rowboat
(Asides upon a great artistic oboe!),

All here together, sent from Rome and Paris,
Los Angeles and London, Cork, and Houst-
On, Texas, by head curator and heiress
And others to whose hands they had vamoosed
(In books or drawers or hung on glassed-in terrace)
Collected and correctly reproduced
So as to give the pure, sweet, overawing
Effects one gets from looking at a drawing

By someone so terrific. What a treasure!
What scarcity of same in the contemporary
World in which so much is "mess and measure"
(In Frank O'Hara's phrase) that when exemplary
Great art like this appears, it gives a pleasure
Which causes one to stop and change itinerary—
Painters begin to paint, and poets write
The new world that grows clearer in its light.

© *Kenneth Koch,*
1972

Jimmy Ernst

The painter who is a poet in his craft is the artist whose intuition leads him always to a fresh and imaginative interpretation of his means. From the outset, Jimmy Ernst has taken the most self-exacting approach to the realization of this poetry. An associational and allusionistic approach would have been natural—easy to him. It was part of his heritage, of his boyhood environment. But he chose a sterner discipline. With allusionistic or anecdotal poetry in authentic expressions in the visual arts always goes a basic imaginative employment of the sensuous means. It was in these basic sensuous means and a tense interrelation of them that Jimmy Ernst recognized from the first the essential poetry of the visual arts, that poetry of painting which trespassed least in the fields of other arts—the imaginative exploration and exploitation of its own materials. This was the poetry he chose to see and to divulge in his art: a creation of vivid, personal values.

> They are underground, the currents we obey.
> Winds of the spirit? Strainings in the field,
> Shifting beyond our guessing.

Jimmy Ernst has felt them; and in his work, for himself and for us, has recorded them.

James Johnson Sweeney
1963

Audrey Flack

To be truly great an artist must express not only a personal truth but a universal one as well, be both specific and general, realistic and abstract, innovative and relevant. Audrey Flack is all of these things, and yet the merit of her work lies not in the compilation of many attributes, but in her refusal to make exclusive choices. She is open to all possibilities and this open-ended acceptance of qualities, stylistic characteristics, and relationships is the goal and probably the reward of twentieth-century art from Cézanne on.

The artists and thinkers of the early twentieth century understood Cézanne's concepts of inter-relatedness imperfectly as a tenuous yoking together of opposites—Symbolism—and responded with the apparently historically inevitable split into the two component parts—Kandinsky's "Great Abstraction" and "Great Realism."

But now, from our vantage point toward the end of this century, we can reassess both Cézanne's achievement and our own recent past. And that is where Audrey Flack finds her place. Her work asserts that we can and must "affirm in spite of," in Nietzsche's crucial phrase—that we can accept the past while affirming the present, that realism can coexist with abstraction, photography and technology with nature and beauty, and that man is both great and small, full of potential and very vulnerable.

Flack's work, then, offers not just the intimate details of her private life, visible in an iconography as rich as that of the seventeenth-century artists she loves so much, or just the universal implications of her political, historical, technological, humanitarian statements, but a simple, clear, and special method for people to follow in living a realistic but humanly rich everyday life.

Flack's painting and photography are characterized by a number of special qualities that attest to her uniqueness in contemporary art. Consummate technique, a strong commitment to figural and still-life representation, humanistic content and a commitment to both the art historical past and current events proclaim her to be perhaps a traditional artist, while her lush colors and surfaces, her abstract spaces and complex compositions, evocative imagery and deep personal involvement with the process and purposes of art reveal her significance in the contemporary art world.

Or, in other words, as I have heard it put, she paints so well, she must be old-fashioned, and conversely, she has so much to say, she can't be very good. But she is both meaningful and expressive, technically careful and powerful.

Flack's diversity of subject matter is unusually wide for an artist at this stage in the middle of her career. From the political paintings of the 1960s, like the *Kennedy Motorcade, November 22, 1963* (1963-1964), to the art historical subjects like *Michelangelo's David* (1971), to the 'vanitas' still lifes of the past decade, Flack has maintained an active interest in human problems and values. This fact alone differentiates her from most of the Photo Realists whose imagery seems sterile and whose main preoccupation seems to be with formal issues and technique. Flack has deliberately chosen to be an accessible artist and is not afraid to tackle "headline" topics, the works of the best-known artists, or universally interpretable allegories. A fin-de-siècle Symbolist would probably judge her work as insufficiently mysterious, yet I am reminded of Gauguin, and Mallarmé's exclamation on seeing his Tahitian paintings, "It is extraordinary that he is able to put so much mystery into such splendor."

Gauguin's struggles to transcend allegory, to paint significant philosophical paintings and yet create works whose formal elements embody his ideas in a significant aesthetic way—what could be termed the union of form and content—are well-known. Indeed a major trend in twentieth-century art has been to repress significant human subject matter and content in favor of form, *or so it has seemed.* A thorough revisionist view of critical and artistic attitudes and objects in the twentieth century, however, reveals that subject and content have never been ignored, just, perhaps, misunderstood. (Witness Kirk Varnedoe's and Robert Herbert's recent and important articles on that most perceptual of artists, Claude Monet.)

So Audrey Flack's position toward the end of a period of abstraction, formalism, minimalism, and conceptual art seems to resolve Gauguin's dilemma by allowing "opposites" to coexist in the same space or context and to resolve the tensions between the intrinsic and extrinsic qualities in a work of art.

Linnea S. Dietrich
1982

Balcomb Greene

In Balcomb Greene's studio at Montauk there are drawings of hands, feet, knees, wrists, sinews and tendons. Here is expressed in drawings as classically severe and exact as anything of da Vinci's the articulation of the human body, here are bones and by the bones alone and the muscles they support can gender be determined, as clear to the beholder as is the sex of an unearthed ulna to a paleontologist. This comes as a revelation to one new to his paintings, or new to them as they were in 1959: flat-surfaced, androgynous and even hermaphroditic, what depth there was expressed in a deliberate and theatrical rather than a natural manner, with mockery often seeming to be the keynote. As in the Chirico, perspective was distorted for purposes that could strike the viewer as cynical.

The studio commanded its own little knoll reached by winding paths through the scrubby growth indigenous to the cliffs out there at the end of the world. The beautiful flat main house with its wide open spaces full of ocean light was a gallery for Greene's disturbing paintings and the smaller, perhaps more "contained" works of his wife, Gertrude Glass. At least one viewer of her work never felt any emotion, unless of course admiration falls in that category. One stood before Greene's work shifting uneasily inside oneself, wondering how a line could be cruel, how a brushstroke could invoke nostalgia, how his palette, then very pale blues and whites and greys, could induce fear or sexual longing. In front of a Glass painting one saw how exuberant this curve was, how mathematical that space; but one was never afraid to turn one's back on a Glass, a remark that cannot be made about a Greene.

There was a period in the sixties—Greene was spending a good deal of time abroad—when his paintings of street scenes, leggy models swinging along sexily despite facelessness, or half-facedness, seemed determined, some said, by an ambition unnatural to the artist; it was as though, they said, the paintings were designed as backgrounds for fashion shows. This criticism was a bit after the fact, as several of Greene's paintings had indeed been used as backgrounds in photographs of haute couture in a slick magazine. If there is one phrase more overworked in the various art worlds than any other it is that one pertaining to someone having "sold out," which generally means that he is making money. Greene was making money; there was as proof his growing patronage in Beverly Hills among the movie stars.

At least in that gallery that year people were talking about some aspects of the paintings actually on display, which must have made it unique among galleries.

But it appeared to the most rabid Greene fan that the search for ambiguity in the canvases—the familiar ambiguity, delightful thought—was in vain. No hermaphrodite strode the streets of Paris; there was no canvas that displayed an effect so disquieting as to simultaneously repel and attract. . . . To some, as one can tell, viewing new Greene paintings was a form of sensation seeking.

Now, looking at *The Boulevard-Paris, 1961,* and *Bicycle Riders of Amsterdam, 1961,* the rabid Greene fan must wonder how he, the fan, missed out on so very much in that show that year. The former painting with glacial girls walking apparently on ice among bare trees, is as faceted as the light from a great diamond; they are the light, they are the trees; behind one model there is a suggestion of a Rockette chorus line of duplicates, though it may be architectural detail. To this viewer the painting resounds with echoes. Concerning the bicycle riders—well, are those not a row of female genitals lined up astride the bicycles at the very front of the canvas? As for ambiguity, *The Cathedral-Paris,* from the show of the same year, is as utterly disturbing as any painting I have ever seen. (I conclude now that something in the air—politics, rhetoric—kept one from seeing what Greene had done, for these are among his most magnificent, but detached, works, and the word in those years was "commitment.") Is it a clown whose ruffed neck and mocking dangerous face fade into and become part of the edifice in *The Cathedral?* Or perhaps the cathedral grows—an idea that I embrace more enthusiastically—from his head, for it is an edifice of refracted light, more Martian than mundane, more Bach than, say, Bernini. Just now it seems to me that the clown resembles Abbie Hoffman, but I am probably only trying to make easy connections.

Or was the controversial year 1964-65? (Such questions complement Greene's work.) True, in one of the paintings the *Tourists* are recognizably so, and *Place Pigalle* is a true street scene in full action; nothing is stable; there is a shimmer of movement. This is also the year of *Bois de Vincennes* which contains enough ambiguity in the woman's face and in the background to satisfy the sensation hunter. This is the painting that, for me, leads directly to the following year's *The Lady,* one of Greene's most terrifying works. Here is a 'lady' swollen with the implications in that word and condition, festering with them, her face gone except for one inward turning eye, evidence of corruption on the flesh of her arm; but her *poitrine* is as *belle* as can be, very Frenchly decolleté, and the clasped hands, if you do not look too close, are the idle hands of a lady. Then, when you go back again to study the painting, you notice that the illusion of *belle poitrine* is just that, for one breast is pneumatic and one padded: the lady has had a mastectomy. Or perhaps this is another hermaphrodite in the painter's vast gallery of this particular ambiguity. (In the painting of which I am proud part-owner, *Double Portrait,* 1958, the two great flat faces, one reminiscent of Charles II's death mask and the other of a figure on a poster left to weather on a board fence, are connected by a string of large floating uneven pearls; the man's ruined mouth is thus linked with the large placid female to whom he is eternally yoked—by what may after all be eggs and sperm instead of pearls.)

If what follows up to 1969—sea scapes, one dark rich work called *The Armada;* another, *The Squall,* as full of lunging movement as a static thing can possibly be—does not belay the anxiety, smug and spurious and New Yorkish, of those decriers of the early sixties, what a shock the seventies must be to them. Here are *Man and Woman; Afternoon by the Sea* with what appears to be a hand waving for help, or in rigor mortis; *Women by the Sea; Shadows on the Beach.* These large sulfurous works, the deathly yellow-green unlike any of Greene's earlier colors, are suffused with eroticism and perversity and a despair that is far removed from the ladies of Montmartre;

Man and Woman makes me think of Matthew Arnold, specifically of "Dover Beach." There is pleading in the bodies which are themselves like remnants of passion, the woman in particular giving a tattered and torn impression. I think that in "Dover Beach" the plea—"Let us be true to one another"—comes too far beyond the possibility of such a thing; it has a dessicated sound, a death rattle like the sough of the retreating sea; and this painting of Greene's seems to be like the very essence of that lost and even foolish hope.

I suppose I am writing now about Greene because for me he is the most literary of painters, his art, and it is a great presence in the world, speaking to me of poems and novels and music (which is, to me, also literary, no defense offered) as well as about painting.

In 1975 I finished my novel *Island People,* written under Greene's pervasive influence, which had begun the first time I saw his classical drawings hiding, in a sense, beneath the ultra-contemporary and even futuristic surfaces of his paintings; this was as responsible as anything else for the style in which I had begun, with *Mrs. October Was Here,* to write. Greene had a show that year and in it there was a painting entitled *Night on the Edge of Town.* This struck me—and who likes to be struck?—as a distillation, condensation, crystallization of what I had tried to do in *Island People,* four long years in the typewriter. I did not have the heart to ask how long it had taken him to paint this masterful canvas. It had been sold and wore its red star with an insolence befitting its star-splendors. Fortunately it is beautifully reproduced in *The Art of Balcomb Greene* and my copy falls open to that painting most readily.

This year, 1982, the Greene show at the ACA Gallery, which just closed on Saturday last, April 24th, contained, featured, co-starred a tremendous canvas called *The Sculptor.* In this a man is forming from his own substance a woman; her thighs are still slightly rough, showing the fine marks of the chisel. The man bends over in benediction and praise of his own body and the creation emerging from it. Just across the stairwell from this there was another canvas called *Hands Moving.* I will not attempt to describe it; perhaps I could not. But more than hands move. This painting moves the heart, the spirit, touches atavism, arouses the anxiety in one and at the same times soothes that anxiety. It is as clear as a piece of crystal and as dense. The colors are royal, like vast chords in a requiem. It made me think of Verdi, of the music of *Falstaff* which is almost all ensemble work, trios, quartets, sextets. But most of all it made me ponder the evolution, if that is possibly the word, of Greene's work over the years, from *The Ancient Form,* pure cubism, to *Blue Space* and

Scene From Molière, through the surrealistic *The Cry* and *The Execution,* for example; through semi-abstractionism and all those other names appended to styles that infuriate Greene so much.

For he is simply a great composer, a great poet and novelist, and a great painter. He moves in Time and through it as he finds new means, or old, of locomotion. He breaks through ice and crystal, drowns in dark seas, is resurrected, or resurrects, on beaches yellow with sundown or the miasma of plague; makes love, splits into genders, self-perpetuating; frightens himself with implication, scares us, tells of the whole process of art and religion in the image of a man cutting from his own flesh a companion-lover-antagonist-god-whatever; and in *Hands Moving* appears to sum it all up. The other paintings at this last show filled the ACA Gallery with light; they were remarkably like windows or worm holes in space leading through to those other worlds: one is disquieted, one is reassured, one is.

His New York show (or Hollywood or Florida or European show) will have canvases that will seem "ultimates," there will be other apotheoses for which one can once again feel gratitude and envy. But most of all, gratitude.

Coleman Dowall
1982

Howard Kanovitz

Howard Kanovitz paints pictures in which the everyday, the familiar, the self-evident, the banal once more become an occasion to view reality with amazement.

I sit in a taxicab that has stopped by the side of the road and look out through the windshield. I see the asphalt roadway in twilight, and the headlights of oncoming cars. Directly in front of me, illuminated by the headlights of my taxi, a large roadsign amid lightpoles with powerlines strung between them, the word "Sugarplum." I see a rearview mirror which sharply reflects, in reverse, another sign on the other side of the road. Simultaneously, I see trees in front of me tinged with the halflight of dusk. I can scarcely distinguish individual trees, only brown-yellow silhouettes in a golden haze. These are not just outlines but masses of color in the midst of which I discern the back of a roadsign on the left side of the highway. Above I see a dense, misty, luminous, orange-beige sky. At the same time as I see all this, I suddenly realize that I am also seeing an out-of-focus rendering in my field of vision of the windshield frame, a portion of the dashboard, the taxi meter, its numerals, the driver's hack license, and an I.D. photograph.

Actually, I don't see all this.

What I'm seeing is depicted in a Kanovitz painting of 1974 titled "Sugarplum." The painting creates the illusion of its existence as reality. The scale of the objects is exactly as I might see them. I am *inside* the painting. The windshield suggests an undefined space in which I sit and out of which I see.

I see a painting the model for which is a photograph, a painting which shows me a unified camera-derived image of what I would ordinarily see sequentially in real life. Which is more tangible, what I see, or what I imagine I am seeing, the latter of which characterizes what I would see if I were *truly* seeing? A look at Kanovitz's image of banal reality tells me of the inaccuracy of my everyday way of seeing and gives me the opportunity to put it to a test.

I will not only test what I see but how I see it. Would that also be a "reality check"—whatever "reality" means? Quite offhand, I ask myself about my attitude as it relates to seeing, and realize that my seeing relates to recognizing. The precision of the image leaves nothing to be desired. But precisely *by means of* and *within* the precision of the image I feel myself subject to illusion. So in the rarefied atmosphere of a museum or a gallery this deceptively authentic-looking reality is proposed to me while at the same time making me aware that this can't be reality but only an image of it. Indeed, an image of an image of this reality. I suspect that this image of reality could deceive me if I let it.

In 1956, Kanovitz painted "Four A.M. Eastern Standard Time." It depicts an early-morning jam session in Kanovitz's Lower East Side loft. The scene is captured in a free, spontaneous improvisation. The eye needs some time before it can recognize the room or any particular details, until it grasps, for example, that the background to the left of the jazz band includes a big studio window opening to a view of the neighborhood cityscape in the early hours before dawn. Kanovitz paints himself and his friends on this canvas, not as an anecdotal portrait but as an atmosphere and mood of a free, unself-conscious, youthful group. (Until the early 1950s the painter was an accomplished jazz musician. He was introduced to art and then to art school by a member of his own band in the late 1940s. He was close to concluding this chapter of his life when in 1956 he planned an extended European trip to see the art of the old masters in Rome, Florence, and Paris.) The artist presents us with a rare confrontation and interplay of two colors, red and blue. He freezes this nocturnal music-making in an almost melancholy stillness. He remains introspective, despite all the tumultuousness of the brushwork reflecting his uprooted inner life. The spontaneous brushwork does not aim at a kind of art that is locked into a static, hermetic, stable order. Instead, it insists on being a direct slice of life, a notation of the present moment, guided only by feeling. One theme is already present in the foreground that will preoccupy Kanovitz again and again—that is the confrontation between inner and outer worlds. His handling of the theme aims to evince internal through external reality and thereby define its relations to the world. In these early paintings he achieves this by presenting an emotionally charged interpretation of figures and objects and an expressionistic exaggeration of their external form. At the same time, the painting is characterized as an ordinary everyday occurrence. But because it is emotionally charged, the unconscious and subconscious are suspended in the content. The psychological aspect of Howard Kanovitz's art is discernibly related to the manner of his brushwork.

Almost 25 years later, he will formulate his statement in a completely different way. Then, through his use of photography, everyday objects will be rendered in a state of alienation, but so precisely rendered that their loss of physical presence becomes visually tangible as they become an almost abstract image of themselves. Simultaneously, the concept of the object takes over the object itself. For Kanovitz it is only in this contradiction that he finds it possible to make the life around us intelligible by means of images. Thus, the nature of the subjectivity with which objects are charged is confronted by Kanovitz in his later so-called photorealist paintings by an investigation of the interrelations between those objects. The fragility of the meaning of things he will make self-evident by establishing contact between those things which in his mind consent to that contact. He will examine these interrelationships when he juxtaposes contradictory elements.

In the course of Kanovitz's trip in 1956, he lived for several months in Florence and while there found Italian painting to be in close harmony with his artistic attitude (which he had not yet been able to put to use in his work). He particularly admired the early Italians Uccello and Piero della Francesca. He studied, visited museums, copied, and sketched. By a stroke of luck, a studio was offered him. An artist his own age was leaving Florence for a couple of months and made available to him what had been the studio of Adolf von Hildebrand, a famous turn-of-the-century German academic sculptor. The studio had not lost too much of its original appearance. Still adorning the high walls of the studio were plaster casts of the Elgin Marbles, parts of the Parthenon frieze depicting the battle of the Lapiths and the Centaurs.

Kanovitz's interest in Italian painting led him to an analysis of Western painting's tradition and esthetics, together with an analysis of the issues arising from the use of nature as a model, in its relationship to painting. In order to deal with these concepts, it was essential that he understand the language and thinking characteristic of Italian painting. What is the relationship in Italian painting of the figure to the background? How is perspective achieved in the representation of space? How does the figure express plasticity in relation to the background while still maintaining its existence as an abstract organization of colors? How, after ardent search, was the new consciousness of reality realized through the innovative painterly means of the early Renaissance? How can space be represented as an illusion by means of single-point perspective on the two-dimensional surface? How can reality be interpreted in the painting and, beyond that, be raised to the level of icon?

On the other hand, in 1951 Kanovitz had been a student and assistant of Franz Kline. His paintings from the early 1950s, of which only a few remain, place Kanovitz unmistakably as a student who is following in his teacher's footsteps. His paintings of that period show accomplishment in form and color, but are substantially derivative. Discernible in these early works, however, are his feeling for color and approach to the problems of space as it relates to the two-dimensional surface and how color values may shift their expression according to their position. In this context we should note, first, that in 1956, around the period when he returned to figurative painting in "Four A.M. Eastern Standard Time," Kanovitz had already grasped the psychic power of color and form as an expression of inner reality. Second, he received this directly from a painter who found his way, as did Jackson Pollock, to a personal statement that put in question the very idea of painting as understood by Europeans. To Kline, likewise, a year in London shortly before World War Two had been significant in the development of his artistic identity.

Kanovitz was thus artistically equipped in a manner contradictory to the Italian painting that had so moved him, and it is hardly surprising that his artistic consciousness suffered a crisis. For two years he traveled around Europe and North Africa. In 1958 he returned to the United States. Almost all the works done after his European experience had no plausibility for Kanovitz, are parenthetical to him, and have been for the most part destroyed. Only at the beginning of the 1960s did he again succeed in creating paintings that he now stands by.

Kanovitz's abstract paintings of 1962 remain artistically characteristic of European tradition while at the same time attempting to get outside of it. In them Kanovitz deals with abstract color/space relationships which occur only on the surface of the canvas. Within these relationships he discovers the subjective imagery of his inner landscapes. If one examines them carefully, one gets sudden glimpses of something like landscape in a terse shorthand of form and color. Still, one never sees actual renderings of landscapes or spaces. These paintings are subjective dialogues in which Kanovitz endows his environment with sensibility. He invents a personal color/space hierarchy and at the same time develops an expressionistic "interaction of color" relating to reality in almost the same way as Paul Klee's "harmony parallel to Nature." At the same time, colors, color movements, and the forms these assume on the surface may stand symbolically for objects, not, however, for their quality as things, but for their spatial interrelationships. At the same time, Kanovitz abandons the brushwork characteristic of "Four A.M."—which was free, spontaneous, rapid, nervous. The new paintings are more ample in movement, more relaxed in composition, but at the same time no longer characterized by frankness, uneasiness, and open-endedness. In these works he regained the centered, self-contained image which holds its own in a universal context, but at the same time stands in close proximity to the European genre of "devotional" art, an icon of the subjective. But this sureness, this cool, lively self-containment and, as it were, tranquil self-discovery also mirrors great inner security. Kanovitz, who never stays in one place, thus also rapidly achieved the freedom after that prolific year to give up what he had won, to "upset the apple cart" in order to strike out in a new direction, without relinquishing the means which he had just fully mastered. He found his way back to the figure.

After his father's death in 1963, Kanovitz came upon some old snapshots while putting the family papers in order. In the snapshots he recognized special pictorial qualities which stimulated his imagination—the frozen moment, the slice of life, the transposition of a spatial situation onto the surface of a picture, the authenticity and, as well, the blurring of real-life intensity. He was drawn to newspaper photographs. These were to have a special influence. He began to make drawings from photographs, and came to terms with the found object, photography, just as he had with any other object in nature. He transformed the photographs in the drawing process and by squaring them up (use of a grid) he isolated units of light value important to the process of painting. The photo dissolved into an abstraction by virtue of the drawing, and the subject matter was transposed as an abstract pattern onto the surface. The grid, once obtained, served as the basis for a cartoon which was then drawn on the canvas and later painted.

The question of figure and background becomes, with the use of photographs as subject matter, the predominant theme of Kanovitz's paintings of 1965. In almost ornamental fashion the figures are woven into the background, which in its technical handling has become even more anonymous—a surface painted by a housepainter. The figure is "realistic" because it is painted from a photograph. But the tonal treatment of the figure has been broken down in such a way that the eye reconstructs it as a "deceptive likeness." In almost Matisse-like fashion, Kanovitz paints, in "Nude Greek" and "Reclining Nude Greek," a bed with a boldly patterned quilt. This pattern serves to describe the object in an abstract color sense while nevertheless depicting it in the anecdotal sense. All this is backed up by an anonymously brushed background which exhibits no further distinctive brushwork, no color nuances. The monochrome surface not only isolates the objects, but is reminiscent of the gold background in medieval and Byzantine painting. The "banal" image undergoes an escalation to the level of an icon somewhere between reality and the invisible world.

The subjective, agitated idiom of the brushwork characteristic of Kanovitz's earlier work is now completely abandoned. Paintings are color/space related compositions, but the abstract has given way to the objective. The individual color areas in the picture are organized relative to one another in accordance with principles of composition independent of their relationship to one another as objects. Although these paintings are based on photographs as patterns, Kanovitz has at the same time come to terms very freely with the original pattern as regards form. He in fact cuts it up, puts it back together, corrects it, transforms it into a collage.

This becomes especially clear when you know the background of "New Yorkers I" and "New Yorkers II." The source was a news photograph of the composer Richard Rodgers sitting with associates in a darkened theater. Dissatisfied with "New Yorkers I," Kanovitz began work on a second version. He revised the content, asking a carefully chosen group of friends to take one or another of the poses depicted in the news picture. He photographed them one by one, made drawings from the photographs, and transferred them to canvas, while retaining the same basic composition. Various significant details were expressively intensified. The fortuitous character of the news picture was transformed in the large-scale composition. The figures are so real they absorb the space surrounding them—it does not need to be represented. Perspective is likewise superfluous. From a photography-based "realism" of figuration we have moved to its antithesis: free, open-ended shape as a spontaneous picture element, a device which, applied in this dialectical fashion, challenges the viewer to see dialectically. "New Yorkers" is a social painting. The placement of figures in front of anonymous color backgrounds serves not only to monumentalize but correspondingly to isolate.

Of the "New Yorkers" and of his works of the mid-sixties Sam Hunter has written: "Something of the ubiquitous American experience of urban loneliness haunts many of these paintings . . . ." "New Yorkers" exhibits a breadth of theme and a depth of content that make of it a worthy reflection of American society; however, the artistic means used to achieve this end all stem from the European classical tradition.

"The Opening" (1967) represented a summing up of Kanovitz's insights as an artist at that time. The photographic techniques were highly refined, he had broadened his collage technique, and these experiments would soon lead to a procedure that he would come to use exclusively over the next ten years: the use of the air brush.

"The Opening" depicts a typical art opening, one that never actually happened but easily could. In accordance with this concept the painting is thematically complex, depicting a mixed crowd in which "anonymous" art-lovers rub elbows with well-known artists, critics, museum people, and other luminaries, shown in groups they would never actually have formed in real life . . . or would they? Thus we find, left to right: Thomas B. Hess, then editor of "Art News," an unknown woman, the painter Barnett Newmann, Dorothy Miller of the Museum of Modern Art, Howard Kanovitz, the collector Max Wassermann, Sam Hunter of Princeton University, an unknown couple, the art dealer Frank Lloyd, Mrs. Max Wassermann, H.H. Arnason, formerly of the Guggenheim Museum, Irving Sandler, the art critic, and Kynaston L. McShine of the Museum of Modern Art.

Kanovitz had photographed them at numerous openings and other events in the course of that year and had assembled the figures from both formal and thematic standpoints. However, form and content overlap. An initial consolidation of the pictures yielded a broad panorama. Extremely significant gestures turned up; only, more often than not, they belonged to less significant persons. Content and formal values were either so unevenly distributed or, conversely, so much alike as to drain them of all potential tension. So Kanovitz went out again and took more pictures. He compared the new batch with those already collected. Putting them all together, he superimposed some of the pictures, made composites and cut-ups of others, constructed relationships that had never existed in reality but were typical and could have happened that way. From all this emerged a first collage. His next step was to ask certain friends to pose in attitudes typical of an open-

ing. Kanovitz had himself photographed in the street, conversing with Tom Hess. H.H. Arnason posed in his office at the Guggenheim. While assembling this jigsaw puzzle, Kanovitz discovered that one figure might be satisfactory but the head wasn't held right. For example, Guggenheim director Tom Messer was looking the "wrong" way. So Kanovitz mounted Hunter's head on Messer's body.

For the color composition, he prepared an almost abstract collage with multi-colored pieces of paper, so as to regulate the patterning, movements, shifts, and overall distribution of colors. For the sake of color relationships, garments and persons were occasionally switched, even sometimes the placement of a given figure's feet, the attitude of a hand, the pattern of a garment, down to such details as a cigarette, handbag, or cocktail glass. The finished collage was photographed, then projected by means of a slide projector onto tracing paper. Certain portions were copied in outline. All this was done piecemeal—fragments of garments, garment patterns, hands, heads, poses, all of which could be readily combined to the best advantage. These Kanovitz transferred by means of carbon paper to the canvas. At the same time color areas were distinguished either by solid lines or by dotted lines or strokes signifying various tonal values. This represented a renewed process of abstraction and analysis but touching upon faces as well as garments, alienating and transforming them into chunks of subject matter to be reassembled solely by color. Large, opaque areas were still painted by brushwork; a face was constructed like a mosaic. Finally, the finished figures were covered with precisely matching silhouettes. The blue background was then applied with a spray gun, which distributed the color evenly over the surface. This created a luminous (one might almost say "optimistic") blue background, while at the same time suggesting a vast abyss intensified by that expressive power inherent in every blue. The arrangement of the figures draws the viewer in precisely because (thanks to the creation of an anonymous space in which the "realistic" figures are enclosed) the scene is being played nowhere and everywhere at one and the same time. The silhouette-like figures anticipate yet another formal development in Kanovitz's work, that of his free-standing cut-outs. The wealth of photographic material that had been assembled in the preparatory stages of "The Opening" had brought Kanovitz in the course of his collage studies to the idea of isolated figure groups. "The People" emerged a year later, in 1968, and in the artist's conception formed, together with "The Opening," a single work extending into three-dimensional space. In "The People," the process of anonymization is developed on the formal level. We are shown only rear views of people who appear to be intently gazing at something in their arrangement vis-à-vis "The Opening," these cut-outs capture our attention. We, the real viewers, are compelled to strike poses exactly like the ones they represent. Like them, we enter into communication with "The Opening," as a painted picture hung in an exhibition. But "The People" also belongs to the depicted opening and is part of that painting's theme. In any case, the reason for the gathering of all these people would vanish and there would be no opening if there were no art to look at. The void would be back with a vengeance, as Hunter called it, "the ubiquitous American experience of urban loneliness . . . ." For us as viewers, this void is physically tangible, too, in the space between the free-standing figures and the picture on the wall. The invisible connections between all of these elements suggest space without representing it by means of perspective.

Not all of Kanovitz's paintings correspond to "The Opening" or "The People" in the details of their genesis and development, but on the whole they do, and certain general principles may be seen to underlie all of his work. The basic fundamental is a coming-to-terms with the world, while maintaining distance from it. To this end he uses as a subject objects from everyday life. To be sure, they are not juxtaposed in the alienating fashion dear to the Surrealists. They are instead invariably composed into an image of reality that *could* correspond to reality. That which does not exist quite the same way in reality is introduced as if it were real and vice versa. Photorealism and trompe-l'œil serve as instruments in that end. The claim to authenticity proper to photography is extended into painting by means of this method. Kanovitz's collage method is therefore not simply a technique but also relates to the intellectual content of his work. It creates not only visual but intellectual illusions, leading us to pose certain questions. The trompe-l'œil becomes a trompe-l'esprit. By painting deceptively realistic copies of reality, Kanovitz is at the same time an inventor of reality, insofar as he invents realities in his paintings, which create an effect of being simple found objects that were copied—therefore real things. But he does this only the better to deceive us.

The line of experimentation embodied in "The People" is further developed in "Mazola and Ronzoni," "Mr. B.J." and "9th Street Junk." Like his contemporaries in Pop Art, Kanovitz was becoming increasingly preoccupied with objects seen in everyday life rather than with figurative social themes. By the use of everyday objects the tension between art/reality and the illusory image was readily generated.

The cut-out figures now stood in empty space not only in the formal sense but in physical reality. What was originally an artistic concept—figures placed in front of a blank background—was now transposed into reality. The background, not cut away, was replaced by the "real" wall in the gallery, in front of which the picture was hung. The reality of the exhibition situation played against the reality of the realism of the art. In the extended series of window paintings, from 1968 to 1970 Kanovitz heightens this contradiction. A trompe-l'œil painting of a window placed in front of a wall claims to be a window *in* that wall. The illusionistic representation, which is a reality as such, puts reality itself on the spot. At the same time the window painting makes no claim about itself beyond the fact that it is a picture. It further emphasizes this claim by thematically restating the question: Isn't the thing framed by the window a picture? Isn't it the picture? This question lends itself to being refined, folded and unfolded at successive levels of complexity, all of which leads inevitably to further paintings. What is the painting? A shaped canvas representing a window with a frame? Or is it what the window frame surrounds like a picture? Or is it what we see behind the windowpane? Or is it the other half of the picture? Is the Soho skyline, with its complex outline of rooftops and watertanks, which are very dark and sharply silhouetted against a bright sky, only an example of how very real reality can appear, regardless of whether it is presented flat or in three dimensions? Or is it an ironical picture element which only happens to resemble a skyline? Is it actually just an abstract configuration of shapes, which for compositional reasons has a place in this painting—because its angularity constitutes an abstract quality to set off the lush and subtly nuanced handling of other portions of the painting?

If Kanovitz paints trompe-l'œil, it is not merely to demonstrate a technical perfection reflecting an art-for-art's sake esthetic stance; it is instead a way of asking questions about our reality and our relationship to reality. The provocation inherent in Kanovitz's work doesn't come from the perfection of his technique, but rather from his juxtaposition of technique and content, together with the fragmentation of content. The abstraction process was linked by him with internal reality, so long as it appeared to be purely abstract. As it would now seem that the illusionistic realism of his paintings cannot be intensified any further, abstraction has shifted to the conceptual complexity of the subject matter. And precisely in the window painting series, we once again encounter Kanovitz's old theme, between internal and external, between inner world and outside reality.

Kanovitz represents this theme when he unfolds

seemingly related fragments of reality only to reveal that they are not truly related at all, even though we often encounter them the same way in reality. He does the opposite as well, demonstrating that things we are not accustomed to seeing in juxtaposition are in fact deeply related. And he does both things without the slightest recourse to Surrealist fictions.

The painting, however, still remains an independent object which sometimes acts against the grain of reality, the better to reveal it, showing the world differently than it is actually organized, although the picture often creates the illusion that things might in fact look that way.

"Projected Street Scene," "One by Threes," and "Composition," all executed in 1971, were exhibited at *documenta v* in Kassel in 1972 and classified in the exhibition category "Questioning Reality: Image Worlds Today." Many critics also spoke of them as "photorealism," a term intended to denote the dialectical confrontation of many artists with photography as thematic content, which could be pegged in terms of "doubt as to the nature of reality." These artists' investigations were immediately hailed as contributions to the definition of the difference between our organic two-eyed vision and the mechanical registration of reality by the one-eyed camera.

Superficial as our experience of reality may be, Kanovitz does not make its dubiousness intelligible by means of exotic juxtapositions. He deals candidly with what he sees and what surrounds him. He takes chunks of all that and demonstrates the multi-layered dubiousness of our apparently self-evident position on this side of the surface of things, ironically enough through a glimpse inside the artist's own studio. Kanovitz reflects the basic doubts about reality that anyone might have and makes them all the more believable by depicting his own private doubts just as he experiences them in the course of his work. He nails them, as it were, by the very act of representing them artistically as an esthetic problem facing the artist in his own studio. As these doubts are embodied in completely ordinary objects and spatial situations, they also mesh plausibly with the viewer's own most private doubts. The believability of artifice is thereby demonstrated. Kanovitz deals with the problem of photography/painting/reality in toto and in the process uses both photographic subject matter and photography itself as they have never been used before. He expresses the same doubts vis-à-vis reality that were formulated in his earlier work, this time with the use of photographs, projections, objects, walls, and traced and painted photographs pinned to a wall. In the process the objects are rendered neither larger nor smaller than they are in reality; this makes it possible to

represent reality either by the object or the photograph. In this fashion, every object belonging to the everyday environment is available to be manipulated and used at will as subject matter. In the structuring of this type of subject matter and in the intersections of the levels of reality captured in it, an element of collage enters into the conceptual process.

In "Sugarplum," and in "Hotel Quai Voltaire" (both 1974), Kanovitz discovered correspondences to this vision of the world in an everyday reality that had nothing to do with the studio atmosphere. What had been investigated in all its complexity in an impressive series of studio paintings was now shown to be discoverable out of the studio, without having to make a scenario of the motif.

An esthetic approach, developed in the paintings "Projected Man" and "As It Is" works in quite a different fashion in the large-scale pastels dating from 1978, which were an outgrowth of Kanovitz's intense preoccupation during the late sixties with drawings as a medium. By the end of the 1970s, Kanovitz had virtually ceased to paint with acrylics on canvas. What with the increasing formal complexity and intricacy of the image content, the laborious and technically painstaking work of drawing with pastels permitted what was actually a more easygoing style. At the same time, Kanovitz dropped much of his earlier repertory of technical aids. He does continue to work, as he always did, from drawings transferred via slide projector to the picture surface. But the still life-like arrangement of objects, or, more accurately, of projections, is first tested on a small picture screen by rear-screen projection, adjusted, and, as it were, esthetically conjugated. Subsequently, the objects projected one by one on the screen serve as a model from which Kanovitz makes a drawing. He is no longer drawing copies of things—glass, ashtray, table, eyeglasses—but photgraphs of them. In the large pastels, diverse realities fall through one another and together. No longer do the things we see make up the theme of the picture. The theme is rather the experiences we make of these things, the awareness we have of them. Kanovitz is at the same time moving in idiosyncratic fashion on a wide curve back to his own beginnings in a psychologically based abstract style. The images interpenetrate, become visible in a flash, sink back again and fade, exactly as the images of our subconscious mingle with the images in our conscious mind. They are mirror images of the internal/external worlds.

Even when Kanovitz is not utilizing traditional techniques, his thought belongs to European tradition. His paintings remain paintings in accordance with our classical concept of what painting is. They reflect reality. Although the medium itself is put in question, the paintings afford a glimpse of realities surrounding us. These realities have found authenticity of a sort in photography, that medium claiming to be a more exact image of reality than the painted picture. Kanovitz, however, subverts the authenticity of photography by introducing it as an apparently unmodified picture element and then raising it to the level of painting. His figurative themes—portraits, landscapes, still lifes—form an unbroken connection with the age-old tradition of painting and are in no way eccentric. They are simply contemporary. Civilization and technology are present—cars, highways, roadsigns, drive-in theaters. A view of the sea shows not just a boat, but a motorboat. We are however most alienated from those landscapes which still have something of undisturbed nature about them although it is always made clear that this is our own damaged, contemporary environment whenever some portion of whatever is still left of nature is depicted. But there is more. Because of our separation from the natural world as represented by a windowpane or car window, we see nature as something fragmented, something we still yearn to take part in but can no longer reach. Here Kanovitz makes formal use of classic repoussier technique. What in Caspar David Friedrich was a rear view of a figure or a rock formation is in Kanovitz the frame of a studio window or a steering wheel, a rearview mirror, or dashboard.

Kanovitz's works often project a feeling of familiarity to me (despite all the surprises they may spring) because he makes use of a European painting idiom which nevertheless mirrors the reality of the New World with American eyes. Yet, Kanovitz, whose basic theme is the many-layeredness of reality, himself remains between realities, between worlds. His way of seeing is rooted in psychology as a theme of painting. It is concerned, not with the image of man, not with the image of things, but with that which passes between them. Thanks to such a vision, thanks to such an approximation of reality which leaves the object alone and as it is, in order to learn its secret, the most ordinary things become special things, and the copy is turned back into an image of verisimilitude.

Jorn Merkert
1979

William King

"The great part of our knowledge of life and of nature—perhaps all our knowledge of their play and interplay—comes to us as gesture. . . .Let us say that good sculpture has a heaviness or lightness which has nothing to do with stone or wood or the carver's trade, but which has everything to do with the gesture which illumines the medium."

R.P. Blackmur

The sculpture of William King is a sculpture of comic gesture. It is sculpture that choreographs a scenario of sociability, of conscious affections and unavowed pretensions, transforming the world of observed manners and unacknowledged motives into mime-like structures of comic revelation. Often very funny, sometimes acerbic, frequently satiric and touching at the same time, it is sculpture that draws from the vast repertory of socialized human gesture a very personal vocabulary of contemporary sculptural forms.

This preoccupation with gesture is the locus of King's sculptural imagination. Everything else that one admires in his work—the virtuoso carving, the deft handling of a wide variety of materials, the shrewd observation and resourceful invention—all this is secondary to the concentration on gesture. The physical stance of the human animal as it negotiates the social arena, the unconscious gait that the body assumes in making its way in the social medium, the emotion traced by the course of a limb, a torso, a head, the features of a face, a coiffure or a costume—from a keen observation of these materials King has garnered a large stock of sculptural images notable for their wit, empathy, simplicity, and psychological precision.

King is, then, among other things, an amusing artist, and nowadays this can at times be almost as much a liability as an asset. Modern art, particularly in its later phases of development, has tended to favor a certain solemnity. Works of art that amuse, that tickle our fancy with unexpected conjunctions of images and materials, that actually afford some

visible and irresistible insight into the human comedy, run the risk of not being taken seriously for their intrinsic esthetic qualities. This is especially true of the art of sculpture. Although the history of modern art can boast some first-rate comic sculpture—by, among others, Picasso, Nadelman, Calder, David Smith, and Richard Stankiewicz—a suspicion of frivolity nonetheless persists wherever wit, satire, or humor plays a central role in the sculptural conception.

Thus, any sculptor aspiring to the comic mode has had to prove himself on purely formal grounds as well as on the basis of his particular vein of comic invention. Amuse us he may—but the comic sculptor had also better do something more than amuse if he hopes to have his work taken as a viable artistic statement. The comic sculptor assumes, by the very nature of his task, a burden that his contemporaries in the more solemn abstract modes of the sculptural art need never be concerned with: the burden of aligning his observation of the particulars of experience with the strictest requirements of form. He must be a connoisseur of two worlds—the world in which he moves as a man and the world of forms to which his vocation as an artist has ineluctably committed him—and he must remain true to both while allowing neither to swamp his attention or dictate his priorities.

In King's case, he has naturally looked to a world of forms that would best accommodate his basic instinct and empathy for the comic gesture, and in doing so has found hints and inspiration, precedents and useful procedures in a variety of sources. His deepest affinity is with the sculpture of Elie Nadelman, whose painted wood carvings and papier-mâché figures—at once so light-hearted, so elegant, so original, and so fully articulated—have provided King with a vision and an ideal of craftsmanship against which to measure his own accomplishment and aspiration. It is indeed a sign of King's own originality that he recognized in Nadelman's *oeuvre*, and did so at a time when this great sculptor was generally neglected, a decisive connection with the nature of his own sculptural ambitions.

In King's work, as in Nadelman's, there is an echo of American folk art, with its air of artisan innocence and its indifference to high-flown rhetoric. And there is also a comparable sophistication, which takes the form of a lively curiosity about the sculpture of the past and an alert attention to new developments that have no very immediate relation to the sculptor's own program. King has lived for extended periods in Italy and Greece, and there are in his work distinct traces of ancient and even Renaissance influences. One sees an Etruscan vision at work in the *Self as Bacchus* (1963) and the ambience of della Robbia in the wonderful series of terra cotta heads from 1959-60. And those spindly legs on which so many King figures are precariously perched—are these slender masses conceivable without a keen appreciation of Giacometti? Yet the classical influences in King's sculpture enter his work as materials for parody as well as emulation, and if Giacometti is a factor in his conception of the human form, and it is because King—who is the most autobiographical of all living sculptors, at times making his sculpture almost a diaristic record of his love life, his family life, and his social milieu—has recognized in his own tall, lanky physique a kind of comic counterpart to the anguished slender figures of the Giacomettian world.

King's own sculptural world is not without its moments of anguish and even misanthropy. The series of cadaverous figures and groups he first showed in 1967—*Greek Restaurant, The Little Dinner, Jimmy,* etc.—were ferocious in laying bare the antics of dramatis personae who were no longer amusing or absurd but denizens of a world already consigned to hell. Without altering the syntax of his figures, King suddenly revealed a new taste for an expressionism of extreme emotions.

But this series has—so far—remained an exception to the general climate of feeling that one finds in King's work. The characteristic King figure may be awkward and even ridiculous, caught unaware in the unlikely contraption of his own physique and decked out with accoutrements that only succeed in amplifying an innate absurdity. His actions may be ungainly, his emotions confused and unacknowledged, his relation to the world at large a farrago of misconceived ideas. But by and large, the world in which this figure exists is very gently envisioned. King is a sharp observer, but also a sympathetic one. There is a marvelous delicacy even in his most satiric images. This is not the kind of comic vision that seeks to humiliate the species.

Nowhere is King's fundamental sociability more evident than in the new series of constructed aluminum structures which he has just completed. These are, in conception at least, open-air sculptures. They have a large, robust, outdoor reach. And they must be just about the friendliest, least daunting, least impersonal open-air sculptures of real quality since Calder designed his first outdoor stabiles.

Not the least interesting thing about this new series is the perspective it affords on King's work as a whole. He is working here in a new material—aluminum plate that is sawed into silhouettes and slotted to allow for easy assemblage. The method is thus a synthesis of carving and construction. The use of this new material—and the scale on which it is used—marks a notable advance in King's development. Gone are the associations that inevitably attach to bronze casts and the carved block of wood. There is a freshness, a leanness, a suggestion of expression unencumbered by associations with other times and other places that King's work has not always enjoyed in the past. The essential gesture embodied in each form is realized with a greater economy, the governing emotion is distilled in a tighter, simpler image.

One is reminded, seeing this new material used with such effortless authority, of the audacity King has shown in his use of materials in recent years. Though fundamentally a carver, he has used burlap and vinyl with a grace and elegance unsurpassed by any other sculptor of his time. Indeed, no other sculptor has moved from the traditional uses of bronze and wood to the new "soft" materials with so little change in the spirit of his work. The very character of his sociable imagery has permitted radical transitions in material and scale without any violence to the spirit of his enterprise.

This imagery persists in the new aluminum sculptures. Figures point, kiss, ponder, reach, sit, crawl, or lie about, their emotions very gently defined. There remains a strong element of the autobiographical; there is no mistaking the fact that the artist is disclosing some personal item of experience. There is a fine intimacy of feeling in these works. But there is also something else—a kind of abstraction or concentration of the gesture that informs them. They are starker, more direct, less obviously ingratiating. The distance between ends and means is now shorter than it was. There is a succinctness in this new work that elevates it above its thematic materials, endowing each image with the suggestion of a good-humored archetype. The last traces of caricature have been transformed into gestures that signify the stages of human experience. There is a concision that seems itself a distillation of experience.

King's talents have always drawn their strength

and energy from a sympathetic, if disabused, perception of the world around him. Among the sculptors of his generation, he has been remarkable in his fidelity to such perceptions—and his ability to create out of his encounter with worldly experiences sculptural images of such economy and probity. There is a quality that is almost Chaplinesque in King's work—a mockery that remains sweet to the taste, a satirical vision that does not exempt the artist himself from the reach of its criticism. He is an artist of uncommon intelligence and originality who has kept sculpture alive—kept it vital and inventive as well as amusing and telling—as a medium of humanistic discourse. At the present moment there is—quite literally—no one else like him.

Hilton Kramer
1982

Lee Krasner

At the center of the artistic upheaval that made New York the art capital of the world in the late nineteen-forties and early fifties were Jackson Pollock and his wife, Lee Krasner, an intense forceful woman with steady grey-blue eyes reflecting her carefully tended independence. Their painting style—Abstract Expressionism—with its revolutionary use of physical gesture, bold images, and rich painterly surfaces made a wide sweep of the then prevailing European Cubist esthetic. What Paris had been to American writing in the twenties, New York suddenly became to American painting in the 'forties and 'fifties. But, unlike Zelda Fitzgerald and the wives of many other American men in the art-and-literary world between the World Wars, Lee Krasner was her own woman, an artist.

Although much curiosity, much speculation surround the formidable personality of Lee Pollock, the widow of the great American painter, very little is known about Lee Krasner, the artist who fought the same battles, exhibited in the same galleries, and painted side by side with her famous, now legendary, husband. For me, as well as many other critics, Lee Krasner is one of the significant painters of the twentieth century—an artist whose importance is only now beginning to be seen.

When I asked Lee Krasner why she was not one of the "Irascible Eighteen," the now famous group of New York School artists who signed a petition in the 'forties—precipitating one of the most notable controversies ever stirred up about American painting—a petition protesting the virtual absence of American art in The Metropolitan Museum of Art in New York, she answered, "I wasn't asked to sign. Barney Newman [the organizer of the protest, Barnett Newman, the outstanding American painter who died in 1970] called, and when I answered the phone, he asked for Jackson. He didn't even bother to inform me of the protest."

And so it went, until recently—when Lee Krasner the painter began to replace Mrs. Jackson Pollock as a public personality.

The Pollocks and their marriage were, and are, their own untold story. Despite his image as the *macho* he-man, Pollock treated Lee Krasner as an equal, a serious professional artist whose work he admired. In her home, Lee Krasner was at least as much painter and comrade-in-art as wife. It turns out that, in fact, Pollock was the only major American artist of the great 'forties to marry another avant-garde artist of his generation.

And Pollock, alone among the patriarchal Abstract Expressionists, investigated the myths of female creativity, painting feminine archetypes (like "The She-Wolf" and "Pasiphaë"), totems, and symbols to balance the masculine principle. While his contemporaries, for the most part, turned to Freud for inspiration, Pollock preferred Jungian subject matter, subject matter that gave equal if not greater emphasis to earth goddesses and the primal creativity of the feminine.

Pollock was not afraid of strong women and Lee Krasner was one of the most courageous, outspoken, and tenacious women any man might have chosen. In many respects, her education was better than Pollock's. A New Yorker who had studied at Cooper Union and the National Academy School of Fine Arts, she had discovered modern art as a young painter during the 'thirties, while Pollock was still painting the American Scene in the manner of his teacher, Thomas Hart Benton, the Missouri painter who tried to make an epic subject of the prairies and fields of rural America but ended with provincial versions of the old masters. Indeed, many have credited Lee Krasner with deflecting Pollock's attention from Benton and focusing it on the great modern masters. She is reticent on the subject. "When I first met Pollock, we disagreed on many things," she admits. "But as struck as I was by the *revelation* his paintings were to me, still I couldn't believe he was discussing Benton that seriously. I can't say if I affected Pollock's views at all. I know that Pollock affected *me* enormously; I daresay I must have had some effect on him."

As I spoke with Lee Krasner, I became increasingly aware of the enormous inner strength it must have taken to have lived her life as an abstract painter, given the obstacles she had to overcome to continue to paint and to paint what she wanted. At first, she had joined the small number of American modernists who fought against academicism and the buckeye illustration of American Scene painting. Surviving the Depression, she battled to find a style that went beyond the limits of European Cubism, a freer, more spontaneously emotional style that eventually became known as Abstract Expressionism. Whatever the odds against her—whether it was the antagonism of her fellow artists whose wives worked to support them, or the indifference of museums, or later the tragedy of her husband's death and the endless litigation over the estate—Lee Krasner kept on painting. Depressed, sleepless, sometimes ill—she continued working. Recently, she has entered a new phase of prolific activity. Her studio is slowly filling up with canvases of pure radiant color contrasted with big open areas of bright white. A floral image seems to dominate; but in many ways the swirling circular motifs, the sense of a physical rhythm and powerful energy link these works with her earliest paintings.

"I have just given all the Pollock material to Eugene Thaw and Virginia Allen, who are preparing the definitive *catalogue raisonné*," she said with an obvious sense of relief. "Now I can once again concentrate on being Lee Krasner the painter." Lee Krasner's life touches every moment of the formation and evolution of postwar American painting—youth in Bohemian Greenwich Village; classes with Hans Hofmann, who brought modern-art theories from Europe to New York; work as one of the few women in the art section of the W.P.A. (the government-supported Depression work project); marriage to Pollock; and, finally, success as a painter on her own.

Today, Lee Krasner lives during the summer in the Long Island house she shared with Pollock in Springs in East Hampton, New York. During the winter, she paints in a studio in her large light-filled apartment on Manhattan's upper East Side. It was there in her living room, surrounded by the plants, shells, rocks, and unusual *art-nouveau* pieces that have much in common with the circling organic forms of her paintings, that I spoke with her about her forty-year career as a woman artist and her experiences, bitter and sweet, as the wife of the man often considered America's greatest painter.

ROSE: Was it hard to be a woman artist in the 'thirties, 'forties, and 'fifties?

KRASNER: I never got any very positive responses to my work. When I met Hans Hofmann, he said, "Zis is so good you would not know it was done by a woman"—meaning the highest compliment he could pay me. That was always there, maybe it will be for a long time. It's as old as Judeo-Christianity. In Western thought—not Eastern—the God image is a male concept and there isn't much room for the female. Those are facts not to be denied. I had an awareness of this way back, somewhere when I was studying at Cooper Union. But it didn't hit me too hard until the recent women's movement. Now, there is an attempt to get a number of women on the scene. For me, it comes a little late.

Q: Yet you have described Pollock's attitude toward your work as very supportive. That he was willing to make provisions for your being an artist must have been important.

A: I don't know how I would have felt if he'd said, "I don't want you to paint," or acted it out in some way. The issue, of course, never arose; but it's inconceivable to me that I would have stopped painting if my husband hadn't approved. Since Pollock was a turbulent man, life with him was never very calm. But the question—should I paint, shouldn't I paint—never arose. I didn't hide my paintings in a closet; they hung on the wall next to his. Since his death, of course, being "Mrs. Jackson Pollock" has become something of a burden—an art-world burden that is. It was never that while Pollock was alive.

Q: I was amazed to hear you say Pollock would wash the dishes if necessary. That image goes so much against the stereotype of Pollock, the two-fisted all-American cowboy, invented by male critics and journalists.

A: Jackson always did the baking. If he wanted apple pie, he baked it. I didn't know how to bake. I usually cooked—but he cooked, too. He also did other necessary household chores. Perhaps if we'd had more money, we would have hired people to do things. But we didn't, so we had to do everything ourselves, and we shared the work.

Q: Is it strange to have witnessed *The Triumph of American Painting* (Irving Sandler's title for his book on the New York School), to have lived through the desperation and struggle, and finally to have seen victory and the fruits of victory?

A: I feel what has happened is quite fantastic. How did it quickly cycle into a scene so foreign ... what happened? In the fifties, there was still vitality and warmth in the art world—it was alive and meaningful. In the 'sixties, I don't know what happened. It wasn't *that* long ago that Arshile Gorky didn't have a gallery, de Kooning didn't have a gallery. Who had galleries? Now overnight, young artists have whole museums. A mushroom can't blow up that fast!

Q: You were among the very first Americans to understand the greatness of Picasso, Matisse, and Mondrian while your contemporaries were still painting the American Scene. But you seem to have had a realization of what was mainstream, of what counted, long before others. . . .

A: Not before Gorky!

Q: How did you feel about the kind of art the Whitney Museum showed in the 'forties?

A: I felt it was pretty depressing. By definition, it is the American Whitney. And I can't be an American anything. Art is art no matter where it is. When it's happening in Paris, you acknowledge that. The last argument I had on this subject was with Mr. Clement Greenberg about the phrase "American-type painting." It offends me. The minute you send up a slogan, you can put anything in the bag and the slogan carries it. That's boring and provincial in thought and concept, and the antithesis of what I mean by art.

Q: Do you feel the same about the new feminist movement? Perhaps the attempt to isolate "feminine" subject matter is as foolish as isolating "American-type" painting.

A: I don't know what's meant by "feminine" subject matter, any more than I understand what's meant by "masculine" subject matter. I'm sympathetic to the women's movement, but I could never support anything called "American" art.

Q: Aside from Mondrian, Picasso, and Matisse, who were you most affected by?

A: Pollock, of course. After meeting Pollock, I gave up the model and still life. I began with a blank canvas and nothing in front of me. Trying to break up the Cubist grid, I started covering the canvas with paint until there was a pile-up of grey matter. This didn't change until I began the Little Image paintings after we had finished cleaning up the house in Springs in 1946. In Pollock, I felt a force that once more moved me as strongly as the impact of Matisse or Picasso.

Q: When did you and Pollock move to Long Island?

A: In November, 1945. We had visited in East Hampton with some friends the previous summer. It was very beautiful, and we had heard that rents were cheap during the winter. I said, "Why don't we rent the place on Eighth Street"—we were living then in a top floor that had a studio on either end and an apartment in between—"and take some canvas and books and try it out in the country for a winter?" Jackson's response was, "Have you gone nuts? Leave New York?" I decided I must have gone nuts. I didn't know where the thought came from. He was proba-

bly right, it was crazy to leave the city. But Jackson had a delayed reaction. Two or three weeks later, he said, "We're going out there and buy a house and we are going to give up New York." Then my reaction was that *he* had flipped his lid. Buy a house on what? We had about forty dollars between us. Finally we did buy the house I'm still in now. The barn was originally directly behind the house. We moved it so it wouldn't block off the view of the marshes, and it became Pollock's studio.

Q: And where did you paint?

A: We arrived in Springs during a northeaster— what an entrance! The house was stuffed with the belongings of people who had lived there. It was a rough scene. The barn was packed solid with cast-iron farm tools. So it was a matter of cleaning everything out before either of us could work. In the meantime, Jackson took one of the bedrooms to try to paint in. When we finally moved the barn and cleaned it out, Jackson began painting there and I worked in the bedroom. We were so busy for about two years tearing off wallpaper and burning up the contents of the house that we didn't have time to do much else. I began making the mosaic table you like because I couldn't work.

Q: Did you look at each other's work and offer criticism?

A: Only by polite invitation to each other's studios. I always responded to his invitation. Sometimes I had to invite him three times to come to mine, but he eventually did come. I always admired what I saw in his studio; I never said, "Change that corner" or "clip that edge." The last time he came to my studio was just before I left for Europe in 1956. (It was my first trip to Europe.) I had just finished a painting called "Prophecy." He said, "Fine. Leave it alone. Except for this," and he pointed to one spot where I had scratched with the back of the brush in wet paint a form like an eye. He advised me to take it out. I thought it was all right and I left it in.

Today, many more American women are choosing Lee Krasner's life-style and her commitments; but to pioneer took a special kind of courage. As her paintings are visionary statements providing mysterious insights into the inner life of an artist, so, too, is Lee Krasner a visionary and a revolutionary personality as a woman.

In 1965, the first breakthrough of recognition for her work came in a retrospective show organized by Bryan Robertson at London's Whitechapel Gallery, one of the most influential public galleries in Europe, an exhibition that was widely praised in the English press. It remains, however, for America to acknowledge that Lee Krasner's works share the same esthetic, the same content, the same history and are of the same quality as those of her male colleagues, the "first generation" New York painters.

Perhaps, because these painters called themselves "heroic," and because we as a people are slower to honor our heroines than our heroes, this recognition has been unnecessarily delayed. But, throughout our history, we have had brave, self-reliant American women who struck out on unknown paths. Lee Krasner is one of them.

Barbara Rose
1972

Ibram Lassaw

Few artists have made more personal and poetic statements in sculpture out of the collective impulse of abstract expressionism than Ibram Lassaw. Yet, of the major figures who emerged during the heroic post-war years of the American avant-garde, he has maintained the most consistent theoretical basis for his art, drawing on such intellectual sources as Taoist and Zen teachings, the psychology of Jung, and other esoteric wisdoms that generally throw light on nonrational mysteries and the creative potencies in man. The ideal calm which Lassaw's personal presence radiates is an achieved and mastered serenity, which never fails to make a striking impression; in his daily life it is disrupted only by regular bouts of energetic creation, and by a continuous sense of astonishment and delight at the inexhaustible spectacle of the world, or more accurately, of the cosmos. Nature continuously and reliably upholds for him an elaborate sense of a purposive universe; and his art has become a simulacrum of that revealed order and purpose, which he can argue in verbal discourse with an almost professional philosophical detachment. He is a man, it appears, who has resolved his struggles and conflicts. Similarly, his art seems attuned only to harmonious forces, but without opening itself to the charge of vapid mysticism.

Like the finest contemporary work of his generation, Lassaw's sculpture is committed to the concrete, thus placing itself firmly within the mainline tradition of modernist abstraction, and perhaps even more relevantly within the episode of abstract expressionism. The expressionist indulgences and wilder, ego-centered gestures of that movement are apparently foreign to his controlled temper, and refined lyrical accents. But there are profound affinities both of style and intellectual content with the generation of David Smith, Pollock and de Kooning, based on a shared sense of personal authenticity, and existential truth, which are given definition in the art of creation. Lassaw's existential convictions are the occasion for celebration rather than sturm-und-drang or of the confessional, and this lends his work its special qualities of undistracted inwardness and exquisite formal poise.

Two aspects of Lassaw's position and achievement reward particular attention: his always vividly expressed and systematic philosophy of creation, and his coherent evolution over three decades as a pioneer in American vanguard art. Most intellectualizations of art miss the mark by losing touch with their object as material expression. At some point the high-sounding phrase fails to ignite our sensuous responses, and it may even obfuscate or replace them. Lassaw's thought is vivid and actual, a running thread of discourse shaped by concrete aesthetic experience and illuminating it, or so it seems after a heady verbal exchange with him, for he is skilled and persuasive in dialectics with as keen a sense of paradox as a Zen master. He attended courses with Suzuki at Columbia in the early fifties, and his growing attraction to Zen teachings stemmed from the conviction that they best explained the phenomenon of art precisely by circumventing the usual conceptualizations of philosophy and getting down to cases in direct, unmediated experience. As he put it, both Zen and modern art "awake us to the present moment." It is no accident that his sculptures bear such titles as *Maintenant* and *Eden Now*. This rapt summons to live in the here and now coincided with the discovery by the action painters in the late forties of the transforming value of "the act of painting" itself, which gave new content to art and freed the American artist from the rigors of an increasingly academic geometric abstraction. Art interpreted through Zen insights also encouraged Lassaw to express his natural wonder and enthusiasm for experience. In his inimitable words, it gave him "a ringside seat, actively participating in the creation of the world." One of his favorite quotations is from Bishop Pike: "The search an artist experiences in the process of creating something, the struggle for ultimate understanding, is inherently religious."

The vast majority of artists would probably find such sentiment unenlightening, or simply too unworldly to credit. Yet there have been a surprising number of the pioneer moderns, notably Mondrian and Kandinsky, who rather innocently embraced religious thought, and even took up a discredited spiritualism to support what was then considered the esoteric pursuit of a non-representational art. Lassaw's personal quest better reconciles spirit and matter, by taking account of the palpable materiality of the work of art. Significantly, his philosophical interests flowered in the intellectual atmosphere of the fifties and only after the establishment of new modes of direct welding in open metal sculpture, within the community of the abstract expressionists.

Lassaw has probably been a respected member of more significant professional associations and movements, from the American Abstract Artists group founded in the thirties, to the "Artist's Club" of recent history, than any American artist since Ad Reinhardt—who once boasted of having been an avant-garde artist for thirty years. He began to work abstractly as early as 1931, in drawings, and was welding open-form sculpture by 1933, although not conclusively in his own stylistic terms. His *Sculpture in Steel* of 1938 is a cage construction with frond-like forms projections from simulated rafter, post, and platform in three different directions. It is today still a most refreshing and original sculpture, as was readily apparent when the Whitney Museum recently displayed the work in an interesting revival of thirties' art in America. It was surely one of the most elegant and controlled expressions of a new kind of drawing in space, with welded metals, of its period. This early work also illustrates a preoccupation with competing geometric and biomorphic formal systems which was to persist throughout the artists' career. Lassaw has always felt the need to breathe new life into the constructivist tradition by fusing it with organic forms, forms generated with more spontaneity than geometric abstraction normally permitted. Some of his other surprisingly mature, and even prophetic, experiments in new form and media have been classified by the artist himself in a statement for the English magazine, *Leonardo*. It provides an intriguing inventory of past modes which very often hint at the artistic directions of the sixties:

Brazing, 1937. Using a discarded refrigerator motor, a compressor and city gas, I succeeded in brazing together iron rods to which I fastened carved wooden shapes. The rods were painted with enamel colors, the wood was painted white.

Shadow boxes, about 1938. There was a series of wooden shadow boxes, each with a light inside, concealed from direct view. In some were painted metal shapes; in others, wires or wooden forms.

Acrylic plastic, 1943. There follows in the work of the next few years a number of steel and plastic constructions. The stainless steel three-dimensional framing was set with shapes made of half-inch-thick lucite. The colors were obtained by applying dye directly to the surface. During 1948, I made some sculptures entirely of intersecting planes of plastic.

Wire structures, 1950. I covered wire with sheet copper and then coated it with solder, building up texture and modelling.

It is always tempting to reconstruct and revise controversial priorities in the development of artistic innovation. The usual test in assigning individual responsibility for change is how consistently an artist has built upon a particular discovery—that is, how decisive to his own development some formal experiment ultimately proved to be. Lassaw is an interesting exception that proves a different rule however. His work of the thirties to a degree anticipated current media experiment in plastics and simple cage-like, "primary" structures, not to mention the welding techniques of the forties. While he did not conclusively achieve a mature, personal style on his own terms until 1951, by touching all bases so early, as it were, in his abstraction of the thirties, he suggests that in a properly interacting and responsive artistic community what may finally emerge as fundamental change in a single spectacular career is part of a shared impulse. It is the sum of many tentative and courageous experiments by numerous fellow-artists who may find they enjoy less dramatic public notice than one or two lionized avant-garde leaders. David Smith and a few other welder-sculptors had already begun to make major reputations for themselves by the late forties, but Lassaw, despite his "centrality" to current modes of innovation, did not arrive at a decisive individual manner until 1950. His sculpture *Milky Way* was the significant turning point of that year, and opened a new line of development for him. It represents an original idiom of space writing in metal, combining the fluencies and fragilities of Pollock's skeins of flung paint with the tough, residual structuralism, and architectonic bias of constructive tradition. The air of tentativeness which that sculpture embodies, its clear rejection of speed of execution or blind impulse, and the searching, slow evolution of its forms establishes relationships between Lassaw's work and the painting of Philip Guston, who also emerged in the early fifties. Both were fine lyricists, and seemed intent on reinstating a more considered and structurally articulated art in place of the facile gestures of action painting that were already becoming shallow and academic cliches. While both these artists conveyed a deceptive air of modesty in their work, they also managed to encompass profound existential truths and meanings, and they brought an extraordinary formal richness to the inexhaustible variations which they played and their chosen abstract motifs.

Milky Way, however, was technically awkward and contrived, with its plastic mixture dripped and built up on a metal armature. The next year Lassaw bought expensive welding equipment, after his first success with sales, and he then began to work in his characteristic manner. Using alloys of bronze, brass and nickel silver, as well as chemicals, he created a permanent palette of colors ranging from burnished gold to corrosive acidulous greens and rusty magentas of somber brilliance. The more deliberate his artifice, curiously, the more his works succeeded in looking like natural mineral formations. During five busy and productive years after 1951, he evolved his basic repertory of formal types: exquisite linear space structures in three dimensions, tersely diagrammatic and entirely diaphanous, of which Philip Johnson's dazzling *Clouds of Magellan* is a luminous example; then came coral-like accretions of nubbly forms, awkward stems sprouting a strangely haunted undersea vegetation of lacy shape and delicate hue; these were followed by box structures made of layers of winding metal foil, cut and torn by interior windows, rather like a Chinese puzzle or surrealist nest of boxes. *Equinox,* a monumental sculpture of the early sixties, best illustrates the last, climactic phase that began in the mid-fifties and completes the quartet of formal types. It is composed of what the artist calls "volumes," sheets of bronze or brass which have been bent and hammered into massive pelvic shapes, and then built up by brazing their surface with deposits of molten and burnished alloys whose brilliance counters the massive hulking forms. This phase represents Lassaw's most monumental style, a period of great impressiveness, strong in its inventive capacity.

The directions established in the early years of the fifties have persisted through the sixties, with rich variations and new technical discoveries. There now seems an almost grave and immutable air of permanence and stability to Lassaw's sculptures, and they give one the sense of having passed from the tenuous order of esthetics to a natural and organic sphere. Recent works like the imposing *Space Densities,* or the more lyrical and freely made *Caryatids,* are demonstrably individual, stamped with their own distinct personality. And yet they stand apart from their creator, as all completely realized art of objective standard ultimately must, with their own distinctive bloom and fullness of existence. They insinuate themselves on our consciousness, first, by their delicate tension and beauty as structure and surface; then, as a mode of awareness, and finally, and perhaps most persistently, as the plausible flora and fauna of a new world. The new works, in fact, seem to exist botanically, part of the organic life process as much as by force of visible artistic will. They have a way of taking on the aspect of sturdy growths in the landscape of the mind, not unlike the scrubby brush, so subtly colored, fragile and yet virtually indestructible, which dots the ocean dunes along the breathtaking beaches near Lassaw's home in East Hampton.

The pieces in this exhibition are a permanent branch and limb of the finest sculpture of today. The artist, however, likes to envision his work not so much in the context of the cultural order as the natural. "The reality I see before me," he has written, "is a living organism, and I believe all its parts are ultimately in ecological interdependence. I, as a man and an artist, participate in it according to my nature. ... The universe performs its divine work of art with both galactic clusters and sub-atomic particles. Life is enacted moment by moment, an illimitable network of energy transactions." The power and poetry of Lassaw's sculpture is that it can accommodate such a sweeping philosophical rationale and still persuade us that it belongs squarely at the center of the most creative and exhilarating episode of post-war American sculpture.

Sam Hunter
1968

John Little

John Little's art is incisive. It crackles with intelligence and bold variety. It also plays a role in one of the most fascinating periods of American art, in which a generation came into contact with European avant-garde artistic movements of the first third of the century and wrested from this experience a body of distinctive, large-scale abstract works of highly individual styles.

Little was born in 1907 in Alabama. He grew up on a large farm, the fifth child and only boy in a family of six children. The Fergusons, his mother's family, could trace ten generations to their point of origin in Scotland, all of which earned a living from farming. In high school Little had thought of becoming an agricultural specialist like his father, but he was more interested in studying art. At 14, while visiting relatives near Buffalo, he explored the possibilities of attending art school and in 1924 entered the Buffalo Fine Arts Academy of the Albright Art Gallery. For the first year Little studied applied design. After that he changed to the fine arts, for which he won a scholarship in 1925.

A highlight of the years in Buffalo came in 1927 when works from Katherine Dreier's Société Anonyme collection were exhibited at the Albright Art Gallery. Little was very impressed with the paintings and with Dreier's lectures. He recalls works by John Graham, Man Ray, Duchamp, a pink and blue Picasso. "They were very good things. It started a revolution in a teacup. A group of us went back to our classes and started experimenting in a big way. We almost got thrown out of the school." He describes the import of the new work as leading away from shading with light and dark toward creating form with color. "We got the idea of taking into consideration not just the figure but the space around it."

After the Dreier experience and while still at Buffalo, Little discovered *Cahiers d'Art,* the French periodical of current art. Also during the Buffalo years, Little heard of another important voice for recent developments in art, and one who would be invaluable to him: the teacher Hans Hofmann. This occurred through his friend and fellow student, Margrethe Overbeck, who had previously studied art in Denver with a former student of Hofmann's Munich classes. It is not clear how much Hofmann's ideas were relayed by this indirect connection; Little feels that not very much was learned at this stage. He and Miss Overbeck did toy with the idea of going to Munich to study with Hofmann. Shortly after, the University of California invited Hofmann to the United States: "So he came to us."

Little's path to Hofmann was not direct, however. While in Buffalo he had begun to study voice at the encouragement of a friend. "I really started out with music to have a better appreciation and knowledge of it. I got more involved than I had anticipated and studied for four years. But I'm glad I did because I learned a great deal." During his first three years in New York City, where he went from Buffalo, Little spent more time with opera than with painting.

When he was first in New York, he also happened upon a means of supporting himself that was to last over twenty years. "I had a friend whose friend was a silent movie actor and he had passed his prime. He went into the textile business and gave me odd jobs." The odd jobs turned into full-time with free lance work on the side. The free lance work became successful and resulted in the John Little Studio which eventually required a staff of twelve and lasted until the early 1950s. By the mid-1930s it was doing a profitable business in fabric and wallpaper design.

In 1933, Little returned to the study of art. Although Hans Hofmann offered courses in New York at this time, Little selected George Grosz at the Art Students League as his teacher because he admired the "color impact" of paintings of the New York skyline by Grosz which were exhibited at the League. Under Grosz, Little painted heads and figures from the model.

During the mid-1930s, Little was a "Sunday painter." Most often he painted landscapes that reveal an incipient modernism.

At this time, Little also first visited East Hampton. During the summers of 1933 and 1934, he drove out on day trips with friends, one of whom was related to an East Hampton resident. The goal of the trip was not to paint but to swim and to appreciate the quite uninhabited countryside, especially around Montauk. Through his friends, Little knew of East Hampton as an art colony of an earlier generation but did not think of it as such in relation to himself.

During the 1930s and early 1940s, Little worked full-time at textile design. When asked about the Federal Art Project of the WPA, he responds, "I thought it was one of the greatest programs of the Roosevelt administration and all of my friends were working there. We socialized, went out to dinner. But I had gone into textiles and just by fluke I became very famous and was making a five-figure annual income. So I never dared talk about it to anybody. But that was a headache in itself ..."

Little was "thorough in a commercial sense" about his textile work. But there was "never a break" in his interest in the fine arts. "No one even thought of selling paintings at that time, or of even showing paintings." In 1937, Little went to Paris for several weeks "to make clear in my own mind the differences between the period styles." He studied at the excellent library of the Musée des Arts Décoratifs, then quite uncrowded. He also went to the Picasso exhibition at the Grand Palais, visited several of the pavilions of the World's Fair and made a side trip to Chartres, as well as concentrating on the purpose of his trip.

By 1937, Hans Hofmann had moved his school to downtown New York and Little began to study with him. Hofmann had experienced the rise of Cubism in Paris as well as its effects upon Mondrian and Delaunay; he also knew the art of Matisse and Kandinsky. Hofmann continually sought to synthesize his experiences and insights for his students. His own understanding evolved over the years, but he constantly stressed looking to nature and its laws for inspiration, tapping one's personal spiritual intuition, and mastering the possibilities of the medium.

"There were so many things that I needed that were available from Hofmann," Little says. "I think it's most fortunate that I studied with him." The way the "solid form and space work together" and the fact that naturalistic color cannot be rendered exactly but rather through an expressive equivalent were concerns that he "had toyed with even before Hofmann, but Hofmann was such a clear teacher, he could come along and say, 'This is the way it works.' His color idea was exactly what I was searching for."

From 1937 to 1942, Little studied with Hofmann in the evenings, five nights a week from the model, and on weekends he worked from the still life that was set up at the school.

A year after he left the Hofmann classes, Little's art was interrupted by two years in the navy. He had tried to draw, but it was an unproductive time. Of his work as an aerial photographer, he says, "It was not a waste of time completely." The study of physics related to photography "adds to one's understanding of what light is and what space is through calculus. When you figure it out mathematically it becomes very clear." When he returned to New York after the war, Little continued his friendship with the Hofmanns who were just setting out for their summer at the Cape. He stayed in Hofmann's 8th Street studio while finding a place to live. "Lee and Jackson [Pollock] were on the top floor of the same building, so we still had a close friendship."

In the 1940s, Little produced a series of vibrant paintings. Many are abstracted from a still life or landscape experience. Composed of brightly colored interlocking angular or geometric shapes, they often bear titles with universal references: *Cosmic Birth, Transcendental Voyage, Pagan Ritual, Ecliptic Terrain.* For the most part, the works are inspired by Cubist interests and bear a resemblance to School of Paris abstractions.

In 1948, while visiting the Pollocks in East Hampton, Little was shown a charming old house "with the roof caving in," but nicely set back from Hog Creek Road in Three Mile Harbor. He liked it immediately, bought it, and took the better part of a year putting it in liveable condition. At first he used the attic for a studio but soon bought an old barn from the Gardiner property in East Hampton village and had it moved to Duck Creek to become a studio. He phased out the textile business and by 1951 had married and begun to live in East Hampton year-round. He planted a vineyard in the first summer and has had thriving gardens for over 30 years.

There were changes in the art world as well. The avant-garde artists who would come to be called Abstract Expressionists were beginning to have gallery exhibitions of their works and incipient recognition in the form of magazine articles and inclusion in museum shows. Little had his first one-man exhibition in November 1946 at the California Palace of the Legion of Honor in San Francisco and in New York at the Betty Parsons gallery in 1948.

The period of the late 1940s and early 1950s was also a time when many New York School artists' styles crystallized into a new form of abstraction. Little's paintings made the shift to a new fullness and authority in 1952 and continued to evolve throughout the decade.

Asked if these stylistic changes related to East Hampton, Little replies, "I do think that the environment influenced me a great deal because I've always drawn from nature. In New York it would be still life; here, I preferred drawing from the landscape." In 1973, he spoke on this same issue:

> I draw constantly from nature. I find that you have to have some basis. I don't trust accidents.... In making drawings I find that it gives me a better basis for form and the real problem of painting. You form an idea of—not a subject—but of the essence of what you see. I work from the landscape a lot: what you see in the landscape, how the forms move back.... When I paint, the color becomes the main thing.... [What] I use from drawing is really the experience of what I observe and then that's consciously or subconsciously, mostly subconsciously, transposed into the painting experience.

This statement is a very helpful one. While many artists of the New York School have found it productive to work with accidents, Little has preferred to "control from the beginning" the "formal unity in paintings." These last words were spoken in 1961 to explain how his work had nothing to do with action painting. In 1982, he affirms that he felt this way in the 1950s as well. Yet Little does say that the hand can "move quicker" than the head. "You get an idea, but then the hand is apt to go to the left instead of to the right." In the same vein: "These things happen so rapidly that it might be a week or two weeks before I really can clearly see what has been done." While he formulates a plan and seeks to work from the essence of what he sees, he also relies upon spontaneity of execution. He is willing to follow what the work might dictate.

Asked about the role of the subconscious in his painting, Little says, "I think the subconscious is there all along. When I work on a painting and when I feel that it's finished or that it's resolved, I think all of the things converge into one: the subconscious and the conscious and the technical."

When Little first moved to East Hampton he began a series of constructions, all made with objects found along the beach of Ditch Plains and the cove beyond in Montauk. He went there to fish and surf cast with Wilfrid Zogbaum who also gleaned rocks for his own sculptures. Little's first construction was made in 1949 and the last in 1960; over a dozen came in between.

After gaining familiarity with Little's abstract paintings of the same time, it comes as a surprise to see personages in the constructions. *Archaic King* causes a chuckle while *Magic Mariner* is more mysterious. Little comments, "I didn't pursue it that way, but the material itself suggested the imagery."

Even in a statement written about the constructions, Little elaborates on processes, elemental rhythms, violence and specific nuances of meaning more than in his other writings on his work. This statement was written as the narration for a short documentary film on the constructions by Paul Falkenberg and Hans Namuth, "John Little: Image from the Sea."

A group of the constructions was exhibited in a two-man show at Guild Hall in 1955 with paintings by Jackson Pollock. Little and Pollock were neighbors and friends who saw each other quite frequently until the latter's death in 1956. In spite of their closeness and common involvement with art, they didn't talk much about it. "I admired [Pollock's] work very much, but I could never feel that it was a part of me or influenced me in any shape or form. It didn't relate to what I was doing." Asked to elaborate on the difference between what he and Pollock were doing, Little says, "It might not be such a big aesthetical difference. It's the approach. He was using the complex interwoven color spatters. Of course, he came up with a form, but it was more hidden. I always worked with the idea of space and form in relation to color in a more open style, [using] white as a color in a form or a space."

Little verbalized what he was doing in 1959 in a statement for the magazine *It is,* (Autumn issue). The statement is spare and abstract, yet bursting with vitality. The ideas expressed are personalized and at the same time consonant with Hofmann's theories. The term "magnetic field" as a description of the picture plane stems specifically, Little explains, from his wartime study of the physics related to photography.

In Little's magisterial works of the recent decades, the amplitude of space is accompanied by that of the colors. They are pure and sonorous. One often has the feeling that the colors in each painting, if plotted on a color wheel, would make a graph around the full circle, with perhaps an indent for an unusual chord. This range in color could be what makes the work feel so comprehensive.

Comprehensive is a good word, too, for Little's entire career. Beginning with academic training, he early appreciated modern art and gradually incorporated its aesthetic into his own work. The study of music enriched his sensibility for abstract visual form and movement. While the technical demands of wartime aerial photography formed his thoughts about the forcefulness with which light rays bounce off a painted surface, twenty years later he became enchanted with aerial photographs of the moon's surface. In the field of applied design, it would seem as if most of the enrichment came from Little's work as a fine artist, rather than the other way around. Yet his continual involvement with design for architecture must have entered into the conception of the architectural sculptures of the mid-1960s. In painting and in sculpture, Little has experimented with both traditional and innovative materials, just as he has worked in the "assembling" mode of the collages and constructions.

In speaking of his work, Little uses formal terms. While he never mentions the emotive content, he does readily concur that it exists. In relation to other artists of the New York School, he places less emphasis on improvisational techniques; nor has his work evolved out of a commitment to a meaningful subject matter stated in universal terms; it usually contains no figurative or symbolic elements. Yet, in varying degrees and at varying times, his work has encompassed all these aspects of the art of his generation. In largeness of scale, painterly brushwork and dramatic color, it has attained bold refinement.

As Little says, he seeks "the big movements of space in relation to the big forms and how they work together." His subject matter is an analogy of the world that we see with our eyes, from the self to the furthest extension. In his art, John Little orchestrates colors, forms and spaces to embody a fullness of experience and a strong and aware personal vision.

Judith Wolfe
1982

Conrad Marca-Relli

Marca-Relli is both Italian and New England (New York). Or neither one nor the other, but a man who lives between the two. He was born in Massachusetts, grew up as an artist in Greenwich Village, and has been in and out of New York and Rome ever since. Something related to the mood of that punctured architecture builds up in him periodically and prevents him from sitting still. He arrives among artist friends in New York City, on Long Island, in Florida, in Ibiza, buys or builds a house, appears to settle down—then, suddenly, he is gone.

In the early fifties when Marca-Relli embarked on his pressurized city-scapes a powerful nucleus of skill, sophistication and theoretical insight had been forming itself in New York art, though few individual artists had yet conceived a distinct idea of where their work was going. Very soon, however, the mainstream of Action painting and expressive abstraction emerged and Marca-Relli headed into the center of it.

With his entry into abstraction, Marca-Relli's dark, unpeopled cities gave way to masks and mannikins and dynamic flowings of forms; the blank edifices were replaced by outlines of heads, shoulders, torsos, legs, as well as shapes that evade direct identification. Then new images were not, like the architectural subjects, kept under the restraint of natural appearances—the form of a leg or torso could be sliced off at will, shifted into arbitrary relations with other forms, or left open for applications of pigment.

Marca-Relli's depth lay in perceiving that for an abstract composition to be emotionally moving, the management of its spatial relations had to be complemented by psychologically affective shapes, neutral areas and textures.

While his imagination manifests itself in the shapes and their arrangement, his ingenuity is revealed in the multiple ways he has devised for holding these shapes together. From traditional pasting, he moved to pins and staples, rivets, grommetted straps, machine screws, used, together with painted simulations, to form elements of pattern in his compositions. Marca-Relli's expanding repertory of substances and construction devices has enabled him to play variations upon, and continually to enrich, a coherent theme. Through twenty-five years of experiment, his creations have realized means for confronting the spectator with images as wilful and enigmatic as those silent, emotion-laden walls of his early days.

Harold Rosenberg
1976

Robert Motherwell

El negro motherwell
el profundo compacto entrado de la noche

Motherwell's black
Profound compact far into the night

Negro negro elegía
negro con sangre negro coagulado
con la cal de los huesos recortando las formas

Black black elegy
Black with coagulated black blood
With the chalk of bones outlining forms

Bandas de lùto
negros estandartes

Arm bands of mourning
Black flags

Negros hoyos brocales para el grito
negro del eco que devuelve negro
de aguas paralizadas

Black rims open for the scream
Black of the echo reflecting black
Of paralyzed waters

Negro de este país de negro siempre

Black of this land of eternal black

¡Oh negro muro de España!

Oh black wall of Spain!

Negro esquelas estáticos sin aire

Static airless obituary black

Dolor de negro concentrado angustia

Pain of concentrated black anguish

Contraido tirante negro en negro
núcleo negro expandido
negro del revés negro

Black pulling against black
Expanded black core
Black back of black

En permanencia negro motherwell redoble

Motherwell's black tolls forever

Atravesado negro puñalada invisible

Pierced black invisible stab

Llanto negro sin fin negro callado

Endless black lament muffled black

Negro espanta sin fondo
negro lengua cortada sin respuesta
o penetrado negro sin salida posible

Black bottomless terror
Black cut tongue without reply
Or penetrated black without an exit

Negro de maldición gitana irremediable

Black of the gypsy's inexorable curse

Yo puedo entrar en ti negro deshecho en lágrimas
I can enter you black dissolved in tears

Por el negro salir purificado

Through black emerge purified

Por el motherwell negro España libre negro
pobre España

Through Motherwell's black free black Spain
Poor Spain

©**Rafael Alberti**
primavera, 1981

Rafael Alberti
Spring, 1981

Alfonso Ossorio

During a career that has spanned three decades, Ossorio's work has been approached critically from two viewpoints, neither of which is incorrect but rather overlapping. First, he has been historically placed among the first generation of Abstract Expressionists, supported by Ossorio's close enduring friendship with Jackson Pollock, whose influence can indeed be seen in the surrealist ink drawings Ossorio produced during the 1940s. Second, much has been rightly made of the artist's relationship with French artist Jean Dubuffet, whose abiding fascination with *Art Brut* ("raw art") closely paralleled Ossorio's, if it did not precisely influence it. Ossorio's development has incorporated these elements into his work—but it is not, as has been suggested, derivative of it.

In fact, Alfonso Ossorio occupies a unique position in contemporary art, one which has frequently aroused controversy, no matter what medium or style he engaged: combinations of wax, watercolor and collage, white lead and plaster, diagrammatic, neo-Constructivist paintings which used and twisted the physical pigment itself into ropelike reliefs, and, from the early 50s until now, complex, sculptural wall constructions and freestanding pieces incorporating such specialized detritus as bones, glass eyes, pieces of tree trunk and mirrors. The work has been described as "primitive," "barbaric," "voodoo-like." The critical emphasis has been placed almost entirely upon the materials themselves—not by the artist, although he is well aware of their connotations of violence, mutilation, and death—rather on the iconography, frequently anthropomorphic, that subsume them. When Ossorio uses the term "congregated imagery," he does so advisedly, to separate his work from the more popular and possibly inaccurate genre of assemblage, or relief construction. The term implies a *cerebral* gathering of materials, not a celebration of the found object. These congregations are often highly decorative, but motivated by an intellectual—even mystical—concern, rather than a purely visual one. If his colors are violent, and his use of materials visceral, it is because he is attempting to give, in Dubuffet's words, "body to conceptual ideas—to the point of making them pass completely into the field of material objects—and at the same time preventing the real things he wants to represent from materializing too much . . . ." The final product is, of course, frequently horrifying, although presenting more declarations of hope than have often been seen in his work. It is also an immensely sophisticated body of work, "borrowing" from Oriental art, sometimes testing new industrial materials (like the plastic sheeting experimented with in 1968), at others re-interpreting the Christian, and pagan, myths of death and resurrection. Although bearing similarities to the best of *Art Brut,* as practiced by the insane and the imprisoned, Ossorio's work indicates a calculated thoughtfulness that can only come from a professional draughtsman and an artist learned in mythic and formal history. The content is demanding, compelling; it is not automatic at all, but complicated, difficult "to read," frequently relying on a *combinatoire* of a visual vocabulary specifically chosen to evoke atavistic responses and an ordered control that "masks" these very emotive elements through complicated design.

Although Ossorio's style and materials have altered throughout the past thirty years, these concerns have bound all the different phases of his work indissolubly. In fact, he will frequently use elements from earlier pieces in new "congregations," a "reclamation," as he terms it. He will return from time to time to generalized figuration, using a piece of tree trunk or a glass eyeball from another, earlier piece; similar compositions echo each other from separate periods in his evolution as an artist. Starfish, bones, feathers, fragments of anatomical photographs emerge, disappear, and re-emerge from work to work. Past, present, and even future combine, dissipate, and reassemble, in an esoteric yet somehow recognizable fashion, in an insinuating blend of repulsion and attraction.

Jane Bell
1977

Larry Rivers

I first met Larry Rivers in 1950. When I started coming down to New York from Harvard, Larry was in Europe, and friends had said we would like each other. Finally, at for me a very literary cocktail party at John Ashbery's we did meet, and we did like each other: I thought he was crazy and he thought I was even crazier. I was very shy, which he thought was intelligence; he was garrulous, which I assumed was brilliance—and on such misinterpretations, thank heavens, many a friendship is based. On the other hand, perhaps it was not a misinterpretation: certain of my literary "heroes" of the Partisan Review variety present at that party paled in significance when I met Larry, and through these years have remained pale while Larry has been something of a hero to me, which would seem to make me intelligent and Larry brilliant. Who knows?

The milieu of those days, and it's funny to think of them in such a way since they are so recent, seems odd now. We all were in our early twenties. John Ashbery, Barbara Guest, Kenneth Koch and I, being poets, divided our time between the literary bar, the San Remo, and the artists' bar, the Cedar Tavern. In the San Remo we argued and gossiped; in the Cedar we often wrote poems while listening to the painters argue and gossip. So far as I know nobody painted in the San Remo while they listened to the writers argue. An interesting sidelight to these social activities was that for most of us non-Academic, and indeed non-literary poets in the sense of the American scene at the time, the painters were the only generous audience for our poetry, and most of us read first publicly in art galleries or at The Club. The literary establishment cared about as much for our work as the Frick cared for Pollock and de Kooning, not that we cared any more for establishments than they did, all of the disinterested parties being honorable men.

Then there was great respect for anyone who did anything marvellous: when Larry introduced me to de Kooning I nearly got sick, as I almost did when I met Auden; if Jackson Pollock tore the door off the men's room in the Cedar it was something he just did and was interesting, not an annoyance. You couldn't see into it anyway, and besides there was then a sense of genius. Or what Kline used to call "the dream." Newman was at that time considered a temporarily silent oracle, being ill, Ad Reinhardt the most shrewd critic of the emergent "art world," Meyer Schapiro a god, and Alfred Barr right up there alongside him but more distant, Holger Cahill another god but one who had abdicated to become more interested in "the thing we're doing," Clement Greenberg the discoverer, Harold Rosenberg the analyzer, and so on and so on. Tom Hess had written the important book. Elaine de Kooning was the White Goddess: she knew everything, told little of it though she talked a lot, and we all adored (and adore) her. She is graceful.

Into this scene Larry came rather like a demented telephone. Nobody knew whether they wanted it in the library, the kitchen or the toilet, but it was electric. Nor did he. The single most important event in his artistic career was when de Kooning said his painting was like pressing your face into wet grass. From the whole jazz scene, which had gradually diminished to a mere recreation, Larry had emerged into the world of art with the sanction of one of his own gods, and indeed the only living one.

It is interesting to think of 1950-52, and the styles of a whole group of young artists whom I knew rather intimately. It was a liberal education on top of an academic one. Larry was chiefly involved with Bonnard and Renoir at first, later Manet and Soutine; Joan Mitchell—Duchamp; Mike Goldberg—Cézanne-Villon-de Kooning; Helen Frankenthaler—Pollock-Miró; Al Leslie—Motherwell; De Niro—Matisse; Nell Blaine—Helion; Hartigan—Pollock-Guston; Harry Jackson—a lot of Matisse with a little German Expressionism; Jane Freilicher—a more subtle combination of Soutine with some Monticelli and Moreau appearing through the paint. The impact of THE NEW AMERICAN PAINTING on this group was being avoided rather self-consciously rather than exploited. If you live in the studio next to Brancusi, you try to think about Poussin. If you drink with Kline you tend to do your black-and-whites in pencil on paper. The artists I knew at that time knew perfectly well who was Great and they weren't going to begin to imitate their works, only their spirit. When someone did a false Clyfford Still or Rothko, it was talked about for weeks. They hadn't read Sartre's *Being and Nothingness* for nothing.

Larry was especially interested in the vast range of possibilities of art. Perhaps because of his experience as a jazz musician, where everything can become fixed so quickly in style and become "the sound," he has moved restlessly from phase to phase. Larry always wanted to see something when he painted, unlike the then-prevalent conceptualized approach. No matter what stylistic period he was in, the friends he spent most time with were invariably subjects in some sense, more or less recognizable, and of course his two sons and his mother-in-law who lived with him were the most frequent subjects (he was separated from his wife, Augusta). His mother-in-law, Mrs. Bertha Burger, was the most frequent subject. She was called Berdie by everyone, a woman of infinite patience and sweetness, who held together a Bohemian household of such staggering complexity it would have driven a less great woman mad. She had a natural grace of temperament which overcame all obstacles and irritations. (During her fatal illness she confessed to me that she had once actually disliked two of Larry's friends because they had been "mean" to her grandsons, and this apologetically!) She appears in every period: an early Soutinesque painting with a cat; at an Impressionistic breakfast table; in the semi-abstract paintings of her seated in a wicker chair; as the double nude, very realistic, now in the collection of the Whitney Museum; in the later *The Athlete's Dream,* which she especially enjoyed because I posed with her and it made her less self-conscious if she was in a painting with a friend; she is also all the figures in The Museum of Modern Art's great painting *The Pool.* Her gentle interestedness extended beyond her own family to everyone who frequented the house, in a completely incurious way. Surrounded by painters and poets suddenly in mid-life, she had an admirable directness with esthetic decisions: "it must be very good work, he's such a wonderful person." Considering the polemics of the time, this was not only a relaxing attitude, it was an adorable one. For many of us her death was as much the personal end of a period as Pollock's death was that of a public one.

I mention these details of Rivers' life because, in the sense that Picasso meant it, his work is very much a diary of his experience. He is inspired directly by visual stimulation and his work is ambitious to save these experiences. Where much of the art of our time has been involved with direct conceptual or ethical considerations, Rivers has chosen to mirror his preoccupations and enthusiasms in an unprogrammatic way. As an example, I think that he personally was very awed by Rothko and that this reveals itself in the seated figures of 1953-54; at the same time I know that a re-reading of *War and Peace,* and his idea of Tolstoy's life, prompted him to commence work on *Washington Crossing the Delaware,* a non-historical, non-philosophical work, the impulse for which I at first thought was hopelessly corny until I saw the painting finished. Rivers veers sharply, as if totally dependent on life impulses, until one observes an obsessively willful insistence on precisely what he is interested in. This goes for the father of our country as well as for the later Camel and Tareyton packs. Who, he seems to be saying, says they're corny? This is the opposite of pop art. He is never naive and never over-sophisticated.

Less known than his jazz interests are Larry's literary ones. He has kept, sporadically, a fairly voluminous and definitely scandalous journal, has written some good poems of a diaristic (boosted by surrealism) nature, and collaborated with several poets (including myself) who have posed for him, mainly I think to keep them quiet while posing and to relax himself when not painting or sculpting. The literary side of his activity has resulted mainly in the poem-paintings with Kenneth Koch, a series of lithographs with me, and our great collaborative play *Kenneth Koch, a Tragedy,* which cannot be printed because it is so filled with '50s art gossip that everyone would sue us. This latter work kept me amused enough to continue to pose for the big nude which took so many months to finish. That is one of Larry's strategies to keep you coming back to the studio, or was when he couldn't afford a professional model. The separation of the arts, in the "pure" sense, has never interested him. As early as 1952, when John Myers and Herbert Machiz were producing the New York Artists' Theater, Larry did a set for a play of mine, *Try! Try!* At the first run-through I realized it was all wrong and withdrew it. He, however, insisted that if he had done the work for the set I should be willing to re-write to my own satisfaction, and so I re-wrote the play for Anne Meacham, J.D. Cannon, Louis Edmonds and Larry's set, and that is the version printed by Grove Press. Few people are so generous towards the work of others.

As I said earlier, Larry is restless, impulsive and compulsive. He loves to work. I remember a typical moment in the late '50s when both Joan Mitchell and

I were visiting the Hamptons and we were all lying on the beach, a state of relaxation Larry can never tolerate for long. Joan was wearing a particularly attractive boating hat and Larry insisted that they go back to his studio so he could make a drawing of her. It is a beautiful drawing, an interesting moment in their lives, and Joan was not only pleased to be drawn, she was relieved because she is terribly vulnerable to sunburn. As Kenneth Koch once said of him, "Larry has a floating subconscious—he's all intuition and no sense."

That's an interesting observation about the person, but actually Larry Rivers brings such a barrage of technical gifts to each intuitive occasion that the moment is totally transformed. Many of these gifts were acquired in the same manner as his talents in music and literature, through practice. Having been hired by Herbie Fields' band in his teens he became adept at the saxophone, meeting a group of poets who interested him he absorbed, pro or con, lots of ideas about style in poetry, and attending classes at Hans Hofmann's school plunged him into activities which were to make him one of the best draftsmen in contemporary art and one of the most subtle and particular colorists. This has been accomplished through work rather than intellection. And here an analogy to jazz can be justified: his hundreds of drawings are each like a separate performance, with its own occasion and subject, and what has been "learned" from the performance is not just the technical facility of the classical pianists' octaves or the

studies in a *Grande Chaumière* class, but the ability to deal with the increased skills that deepening of subject matter and the risks of anxiety-dictated variety demand for clear expression. When Rivers draws a nose, it is my nose, your nose, his nose, Gogol's nose, and the nose from a drawing instruction manual, and it is the result of highly conscious skill.

There is a little bit of Hemingway in his attitude toward ability, toward what you do to a canvas or an armature. His early painting, *The Burial,* is really, in a less arrogant manner than Hemingway's, "getting into the ring" with Courbet *(A Burial at Ornans),* just as his nude portrait of me started in his mind from envy of the then newly acquired Géricault slave with the rope at the Metropolitan Museum, the portrait *Augusta* from a Delacroix; and even this year he is still fighting it out, this time with David's *Napoleon.* As with his friends, as with cigarette and cigar boxes, maps, and animals, he is always engaged in an esthetic athleticism which sharpens the eye, hand and arm in order to beat the bugaboos of banality and boredom, deliberately invited into the painting and then triumphed over.

What his work has always had to say to me, I guess, is to be more keenly interested while I'm still alive. And perhaps this is the most important thing art can say.

Frank O'Hara
1965

Alexander Russo

Of all the elements to which I respond in Alex Russo's work, there are two in particular which attracted me immediately and which continue to affect me—his sure sense of composition (always inventive and unpredictable) and, what is even more meaningful to me, the centrality of human figures in his work. I find his forms strong and arresting, both in and of themselves, and in the way they connect (or deliberately fail to connect) with each other.

As to the human figures in his work, perhaps "personnages" would be a better word, because the former phrase suggests a preoccupation with the male or female form *per se*, which is not what seems to concern him. The "personnages" in Alex Russo's work, however impersonal, convey a sense of mystery, a sense of the ambiguity of the human condition. His figures evoke poignant feelings in me, sometimes generated by their estrangement from the world around them; sometimes resulting from the unique manner in which they both absorb and are absorbed by their world. I can think of no other artist who affects me in quite this way.

Sheldon Harnick
1982

George Segal

With Segal it's not a matter of the found object; it's the chosen object.

Marcel Duchamp
1965

—Marcel Duchamp, 1965, foreword to Segal exhibition catalogue at the Sidney Janus Gallery, New York.

Syd Solomon

In January of 1961 I wrote an essay on Syd Solomon and his work which appeared in the catalogue of a gallery show in Sarasota which coincided with the 14th Annual Art Symposium of the Ringling Museum of Art.

I said then that "he is deeply involved in and armored by the singular excitements of the progressive phases of an artistic maturity of such scope and strength no man can predict its ultimate reach and persuasion."

I would write that same thing about him today, but I would write it differently. Today I would say, "He knows that he is very good and knows he is getting better. That is an excitement which fuels his energy. Neither he nor we can say how much better he will get."

The earlier effort of mine was too ornamented and oratorical. I was self-conscious about writing an essay for a catalogue of an art show. And, though I had been a professional writer for sixteen years, I had not yet learned enough about the power of simplicity.

At that time we had known Syd Solomon for more than ten years, and Dorothy and I had purchased a few of the paintings which had pleased us. Now it is more than twenty-seven years of being friends and neighbors, and we have acquired several more, and they are a good and welcome part of our lives.

He has gotten very good indeed. We are very proud of him. Great museums have given him exhibitions and have purchased his work. His is a hefty name in the art world.

With awareness that the analogy is flawed, I want to say that he too has been learning the powerful uses of simplification.

With great style, with stinging colors and sensuous textures, he has been distilling his own strengths and needs into very pure forms and symbols. Though I do not wish to steer too close to the buzz-words of much of the art criticism of today, I think he is now achieving a kind of mystic simplicity.

Once when Dorothy and I were in the Whitney Museum she stood close to an absolutely gigantic Franz Kline and looked up at it and said, wonderingly, "It's like standing under a great tree!"

This, I think, is the special persuasion of strength, of distillation, of simplicity.

In the seventeen years since my last essay about Syd Solomon, I have been working the same side of that diverting street—trying to cut away all the redundant bumps and lumps, the encrustations and the dangling ornaments. The things which are not said, in a painting or in a paragraph, but which are known by the painter or the writer, create such a subterranean resonance, they make the visible parts stronger and more true.

In my 1961 essay I said, "When I achieve a subjective response to a painting by Syd Solomon, I suddenly see a distillation of nature, a brooding, powerful, watchful thing, eternally concerned with its own cycles and rhythms, achieving an implacable beauty through a curious blend of inevitability and a total indifference to my existence—except as a helpless passenger on a planet of which the painting is but one severe distillation. I do not 'look' at such paintings. They confront me."

Now I would say it differently: These paintings have a surface accessibility. They have a handsome look. They glow. They decorate. But they are talking another language at the same time, far less accessible, almost inaudible. It is a gut language of ancient visceral symbols. When both these idioms are accessible to the viewer, they pull and push against each other, reacting in such a way that great tension is produced, and there is a simultaneous intellectual-emotional reaction.

When you do not hear that second language, the painting is still a fine thing to look upon. Let us say you respond in that special dual way to one in ten, as I do. Is that not an agreeable feast? Were you and he to be identical in mind, heart and spirit, you would respond to each and every one in the same way he responds—a grotesque improbability. When painting becomes a public language, accessible to all in every dimension, then it is thin, tasteless and speedily forgotten.

It is a process of search, of out-reach, to try to bring the audible and inaudible parts of the work under control. You keep trying to do things which you cannot quite manage. After several disasters, you bring it off. This is known as risk. And this is known also, as getting better. The artist must stress himself to reveal tension.

In 1961 I said, "Without a merciless and continuing acceptance of risk there can be no victories, no failures, no growth. The artist rides a strong horse at a full gallop through an unknown, unending city in the empty dark, trusting his instincts and his control to avoid spending too much time in dead end streets, or doubling back on himself unwittingly, or losing the spur of direction and slowing to the final ruminative walk."

Though that is slightly florid, I shall not change it. Nor would I want to change the way I ended it.

"This has been a most personal appraisal of the man as a creator, and of the duality of the effect his work has upon me. Syd Solomon is a strong and thoughtful man, a man in the midst of life, moving his work forward in those extremely personal ways which feed his strength. His work has enhanced my own awareness of my environment and my historical microsecond of existence.

"I am glad it has happened this way, and glad that it will continue."

John D. MacDonald
1978

Esteban Vicente

Collage has generally been the medium for an art of interruption, of abrupt jumps that break the initial momentum of mood, of plastic structure or of literary content. In Cubist collages, the jumps are mainly aesthetic, from one specific texture, pattern, plane or visual situation to another. In Dada collages, the jumps are from one fragment of reality to another, creating a sense of the bitter or the absurd. In Surrealism (to overemphasize the difference between these two movements), the jumps are from fantasy to reality or from fantasy to fantasy. And these juxtaposed elements, whatever they are, are usually caught midway in an attitude of surprise, like Marianne Moore's "real bird in a painted tree." For the observer, the expectation of what is to come—depending on whether he noticed the bird or the tree first—is dashed by the second sight. The interruption is perpetuated in one frozen moment. Action is caught at an impasse. Collages, to use cinematic terminology, are in most cases *stills*.

In reference to the bulk of the work in this forty-year-old medium, Esteban Vicente's collages are uncharacteristically fluid and animated. Color and forms give a sense of continuous motion, sliding into one another, exchanging positions, continuing beyond and negating the edges of the separate pieces of paper. His technique tends to obscure the fact that he is working with paper. Not only does he make no attempt to retain the character of paper in opposition to that of paint; he seems actually to be trying to disguise it both through his concept of drawing and in his treatment of the surface of the paper, which is deluged with washes of paint or scrubbed with pastel, charcoal, pen or pencil. Often, from a distance or in reproduction, his collages could be confused with his paintings. The aspirations and effects of both are identical. But because he is essentially involved with painting effects, there are several possibilities of collage that Vicente sacrifices to get where he's going.

The carefully cherished patterns and textures of the familiar collage accomplish two plastic objectives: they maintain the flat surface sacred to much modern art, and they fix the composition in a range of precisely limited scales—still-life, interior or human in reference. Vicente's irregularly torn pieces of paper do not hold their flatness, but swoop off into deep perspectives. The surface of the paper has lost its immediacy—its two-dimensional presence—in exchange for a smoothly ambiguous large scale rare in this medium. Rejecting the close-up fragmentation of "classic" collage, Vicente chooses to see panoramas. Rejecting the possibilities of the "frozen moment," he offers, rather, an interweaving of events. The element of poetic shock—to be found in the concept of simultaneity—gives way in Vicente's work to a serenely single-minded and sequential imagery. Forms unfold in one measured procession. Unrelated to any of the specific traditions of this medium, Vicente's collages connect, rather, with painting traditions—of Expressionism, Fauvism, even Futurism. He is not interested in collage except "as a way to get somewhere else."

"Collage is a technique to arrive at a painting . . . collage is a sketch for painting . . . collage is a substitute for painting," says Vicente describing his rather unconventional attitude toward the medium. Concentrated on painting for some three decades, he backed into the collage one Sunday in Berkeley, California, in 1950, because he wanted to work and his paints and brushes had not yet arrived. He cut up a colored Sunday supplement and pasted up a composition. This first collage supplied the motif for a later painting. He has never begun one as a project in itself, but only as a kind of general relief when he is stuck on a painting or perhaps as an attempt to work out some specific area. However, "sometimes these sketches finish themselves." When this happens, the collage means much the same thing to him as one of his finished paintings. Although he spends much more of his time on his painting, collages now make up half of his annual output (about eight works in each medium). Spending months on a painting, weeks on a collage, he has developed methods so interactive that it is impossible to describe one without bringing up the other.

Born in 1906 in Segovia, one of the provinces of old Castille, north of Madrid, near the Guadarama mountains, Vicente decided to become an artist when he was sixteen years old. He quit the military academy that his father and grandfather had gone to, and began to study sculpture at the School of Fine Arts in Madrid. Here he met a "very brilliant guy from Iowa named James Gilbert, very refined, could find values anywhere." Almost every artist seems to meet someone at the beginning of his career who profoundly and often inexplicably affects later decisions and attitudes, someone whose personal expression is identified with the peculiar glamor of art that hits certain people so hard that they are caught up with it for the rest of their lives. James Gilbert, the painter, was the someone for Vicente. They both quit school and began to work on their own, sharing a studio. Fascinated by Gilbert's intense preoccupation with his somber-toned landscapes, Vicente gave up sculpture after three years ("I always made the heads too small, anyway") and became a painter. "Plaster and clay seemed dead when I felt the appeal of color." He began to haunt the Prado. "It was most terrific to see the abundance of flesh of Rubens next to Greco who avoids the flesh . . . the colorless light of Velasquez and Goya." These artists all had their influence on his figure compositions. "Then I discovered that there were certain people in France—Cézanne, Matisse, Picasso." He bought little books of illustrations. He subscribed to Parisian magazines. And he began to get restless. "Madrid was El Prado . . . the past. The contemporary work was unrelated to both. I was looking for air." America had lots of air, he thought, but Gilbert persuaded him that it was the wrong kind. "America is no place for an artist," he was told, and the first words in English Gilbert taught him were how to ask for work—"commercial work." This discouraged Vicente sufficiently and he went to Paris instead, after having a show of abstractions in Madrid at the age of twenty-two. But it was difficult making a living in Paris too. He retouched photographs and worked on stage sets and did his painting at night. After spending several years in Paris, he decided "the whole thing was too commercial—too businesslike," and in 1936, he came to America to stay—and here, except for a small amount of time teaching, he has been able to devote himself to painting. He saw little thereafter of Gilbert, "who paints and paints and paints and never gives a show."

Other American artists to influence the young Vicente, more concretely, if perhaps less deeply, were Demuth, Dove, Ryder, Gorky—the first artists whose work impressed him upon his arrival in this country. But whether he was working on the curious blunt-contoured figure compositions reminiscent of Daumier, with which he made his first reputation in this country in the late 'thirties, or on his recent abstractions that offer a direct reflection of participation in a large movement in contemporary American painting, there is always a stubborn insistence on private methods that sets Vicente's work apart, a heterodox technique—and, therefore, philosophy—within any style he chooses.

Heterodoxly, he begins a collage as he does a painting, with a charcoal drawing. His paper, like his canvas, is tacked to the ten-foot-square partition that serves as his easel. Then, working as if each step were to be the final one—since he has no preconceived ideas on how full or empty a finished work should look—he applies his colored paper, proceeding from small to large areas "so as not to block the space." Sometimes he decides a painting is finished when the canvas is not completely covered with pigment. And in the same way, the white of the original sheet of paper on which he pastes the colored pieces may be partially uncovered at the end. "The important thing is to keep the sensation of white, the open sensation of white." "But," the painter continues, "this is most easily done by translating white into a color." So, generally, both his paintings and collages are covered by patches of contrasting hues that produce expansive and curiously volatile effects. This volatility results from the closeness of tone which is so uniform that, in a black-and-white photograph of one of his works, two contrasting colors will lose their boundaries and blend in one value. Seen in the changing light of an ordinary day, his colors keep shifting their relationships, becoming luminous at dusk, flat and clear at noon. Contrasting tones he finds too graphic or static, and he prefers the wider play of light when drawing is carried by color alone. "Color to me means light," he says, rejecting the sensuality invoked when color means "surface."

The colors on his palette table are those of the sheets of paper stacked in his cabinet. Lavender, blue, grey, pink, rust, ocher and orange prevail. The shades are intermediate. Opaque, heavy, dusty, powdery, sooty, pale or deep, every color is modified by the addition of others—complementaries or white. He claims he never uses a pigment straight from the tube, but his reds and yellows often flare up with an intensity that seems improbable in a mixed color. The surface of his paper, like that of his canvas, is covered with thin, even washes that register the tracks of his brushes. Sometimes he works with construction papers, but he does not favor them because he often can't get the exact hues he wants, and also because they fade in time. He prefers to paint batches of paper in the desired colors—he uses about twelve here, covering enough in one day to last for months. (For this he uses a Devoe lacquer.)

Pieces are torn out of these sheets and pinned in place. He constantly alters their size and shapes, tearing off strips, substituting larger or smaller fragments, changing the position of color areas. This is done in much the same way that he paints, inching his way around the oddly tentative forms with small brushes. (He uses mostly long-haired ten-cent brushes from a hardware store, just a few good, short-haired bristle brushes.) As colors are kept close in tone, so the sizes of the separate shapes are delicately uniform. There are rarely leaps from small to large. The unit sizes remain more or less constant, and this evenness of size makes for the same sense of expansion and fluidity created by the evenness of tone.

Lines don't figure as contours, but mainly as scratches on the surface of a shape. Thus their action is textural or tonal, like that of brush strokes, not sculptural, as in drawing. This applies only to the final stage. In the development of a painting or a collage, he keeps using charcoal to describe temporary contours which are then filled out or covered with paint or paper. Exceptional are a series of black-and-white collages which relate directly to drawings. The pieces of paper in these earliest collages were all cut out in the sharp, Futuristic edges that characterized both his painting and drawing of three years ago. But recently he prefers the evasive, fuzzy edges produced by tearing. He now uses scissors only occasionally to get slivers of color to wedge between the larger, vaguer forms, or to trim torn edges to a more precise line. In the case of this formal device, it was his paintings that followed his collages rather than the other way around. Now areas of color on his canvas often resemble pieces of roughly torn paper. (Like a great many contemporary artists, he actually does pin on paper in the earlier stages of a painting to try out different shapes and colors—a time- and surface-saving device that probably stretches back to the Renaissance.)

When he is satisfied with the position of the pinned-up shapes, he pastes them in place, and then proceeds to pin and paste new areas on top of them. (For his large collages—they range from 36 by 45 to 7 by 9 inches—he employs "Foxpaste," a water paste which he mixes himself; for the smaller ones, a ready-made waterless paste does just as well.) He used to paste the paper carefully flat, but now allows the edges to rise up, buckle or curl. Thus emphasized, the edges create a subtle shift of planes even when they do not define a change in color. As he adds new areas, a piece of paper underneath may eventually be covered except for an edge. "Amazing the difference it makes whether a form is left over or directly applied," he says, but this observation, he admits, applies to painted shapes as well as pasted ones. Sometimes, after work of a week or two, the pieces of paper accumulate in thick layers; and since he dislikes heavy "impastos" in collage as in painting, he tears off the papers and starts over, just as he scrapes off paint to keep his actual impastos thin and transparent. All through the making of a collage, Vicente uses his brush freely, applying tempera, watercolor and often oil. And over these painted surfaces may come charcoal, pencil, ink or pastel. Collage, in this Expressionist technique, is reduced to a non-ideological, purely physical process. If custom makes laws, then Vicente has quietly broken those of the collage. But are there any laws in this territory?

Vicente seems to be one of the few artists working with collage who is interested in an expression of depth (excluding the instances of academic perspective often employed by the Surrealists). And it is through his management of depth that Vicente achieves his remarkable scale and also his sense of mobility. The scale is non-human, that of a landscape, although Vicente is no longer interested in landscape as a subject for painting. If he thinks of anything concrete when working on an abstraction, it is usually a figure. As a student Vicente was much impressed in Madrid by a group of Goyas, each one limited to four colors, that blazed with the high, transparent, colorless, Spanish light he loves. The artist was a man with a beard, not a child, when he left Spain, and all of the things that he left behind keep coming back in his work. Landscape and drawing, which he pushes out of his art, push their way right back and the hills of the *View of Toledo* here extend into the twentieth century.

Elaine de Kooning
1972

Jack Youngerman

An Interview with Jack Youngerman: The New Sculpture

DB: How do you define the limitations of painting and sculpture in your work?

JY: Most of my paintings go beyond being concerned with a figure floating on ground, and involve interconnected images. Forms are fashioned by other forms which intrude upon them. Figure-ground relationships imply shapes and volumes in space, that is, they imply sculpture. In sculpture, real space completes the form, but the shape has its own definition. In painting, there are definite boundaries to the canvas, but sculptural space is unbounded, infinite space. Sculpture for me is the optimum realization of forms which cannot be isolated on the canvas. I feel that making sculpture has freed my painting in a sense. It allows me to introduce new elements into may paintings. I am more interested now in what I will do with a form than with the creation of forms, and I no longer search so far afield for new forms.

Denise Bratton
1975

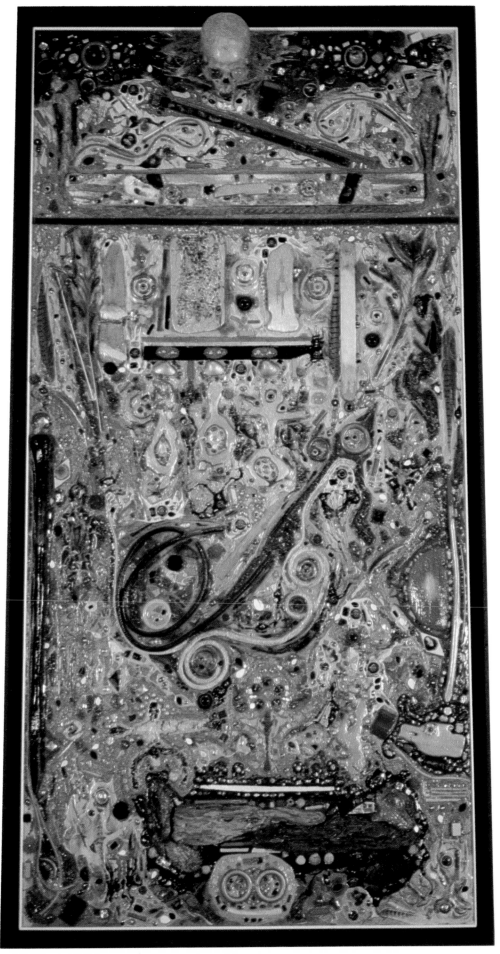

ALFONSO OSSORIO Garden of Eden, 1960, plastic, wood, bone, oil and enamel paints on masonite, 96 x 48 inches.

ROBERT MOTHERWELL Nemesis, 1981-82, acrylic on canvas, 60 x 44 inches.

ALEXANDER RUSSO Age Of Ontological Crisis, 1982, acrylic on canvas, 66 x 48 inches.

LEE KRASNER Between Two Appearances, 1981, oil on canvas with paper collage, 47 x 57¼ inches.

CONRAD MARCA-RELLI Untitled L-13-74, 1974, collage, 59 x 64 inches.

GEORGE SEGAL Helen With Apples, 1981, painted plaster and wood, 96 x 48 x 45 inches.

ALICE BABER For A Book Of Kings, 1974, oil on canvas, 77 x 58 inches.

92

WILLIAM KING Wallflower, 1970, Aluminum, 43 x 46 x 19 inches.

Courtesy Terry Dintenfass Gallery

HOWARD KANOVITZ What Did Bani-Sadr Say?, 1982, acrylic on canvas, 78 x 62½ inches.

94

She is stars in the sunrise   She is flown, so very far above us now
lightening on a sunny day   Over our politics of love
Rain on the ocean   Over the limits of consciousness

AUDREY FLACK Who She Is, 1982, oil and acrylic on canvas, 84 x 60 inches.

JACK YOUNGERMAN Little Huracan, 1982, oil on gesso over epoxy resin on carved polystyrene, 72 x 56 x 6 inches.

ESTEBAN VICENTE Blue Band, 1978, collage on canvas, 48 x 38 inches.

JOHN LITTLE Blue Hemisphere, 1978, oil on canvas, 60 x 52 inches.

JAMES BROOKS   Runge, 1972, acrylic on canvas, 36 x 36 inches.

JIMMY ERNST Illumination For An Absent Friend, 1978, oil on canvas, 55 x 70 inches.

ELAINE de KOONING Bacchus #3, 1978, acrylic on canvas, 78 x 50 inches.

LARRY RIVERS Webster Angry On A Cigar Box Top, 1979, acrylic on canvas, 52 x 56. inches.

WILLEM de KOONING Untitled X, 1981, oil on canvas, 60 x 55 inches.

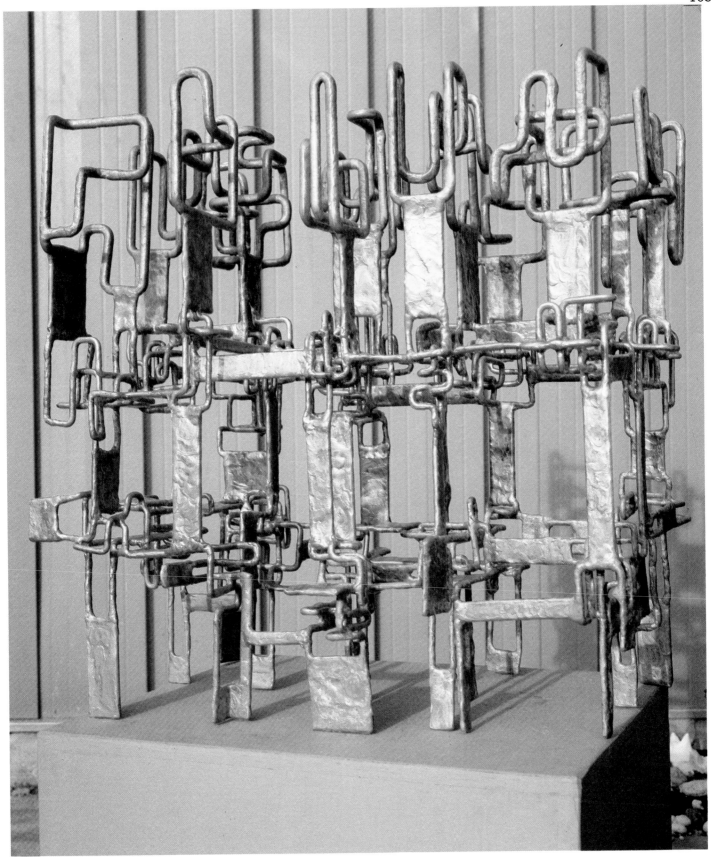

IBRAM LASSAW Metagalaxy, 1979, Bronze, 31 x 31 x 23 inches.

SYD SOLOMON Windworld, 1980, acrylic and oil on canvas, 72 x 60 inches.

CALVIN ALBERT Bridge, 1980, terra cotta, 18 x 18 x 13 inches.

WARREN BRANDT Resting Model, 1981, oil on canvas, 20 x 24 inches.

BALCOMB GREENE Hands Moving, 1982, 60 x 48 inches.

108

CHUCK CLOSE Self Portrait/Manipulated, 1982, handmade paper, grey, ½ inch grid, manipulated and air dried, 38½ x 28½ inches.